Jacques Prévert

Chiasma 12

General Editor

Michael Bishop

Editorial Committee

**Adelaide Russo, Michaël Sheringham
Steven Winspur, Sonya Stephens
Michael Brophy, Anja Pearre**

Rodopi

AMSTERDAM – NEW YORK, NY 2002

Jacques Prévert

From Film and Theater
to
Poetry, Art and Song

Michael Bishop

Cover illustration: Portrait de Janine, 1943 ©Succession Prévert

Le papier sur lequel le présent ouvrage est imprimé remplit les prescriptions de "ISO 9706:1994, Information et documentation - Papier pour documents - Prescriptions pour la permanence".

The paper on which this book is printed meets the requirements of "ISO 9706:1994, Information and documentation - Paper for documents - Requirements for permanence".

ISBN: 90-420-1329-X
©Editions Rodopi B.V., Amsterdam – New York, NY 2002
Printed in The Netherlands

TABLE OF CONTENTS

CHIASMA

Chiasma seeks to foster urgent critical assessments focussing upon joinings and crisscrossings, single, triangular, multiple, in the realm of modern French literature. Studies may be of an interdisciplinary nature, developing connections with art, philosophy, linguistics and beyond, or display intertextual or other plurivocal concerns of varying order.

> soudain le fou rire le prend
> et il efface tout
> les chiffres et les mots
> les dates et les noms
> les phrases et les pièges
> (Suddenly he can't stop laughing
> And he erases everything
> Numbers and words
> Dates and names
> Sentences and traps)
> Jacques Prévert, *Paroles* (1,43)

FROM ROMANTICISM TO THE FIRST WORLD WAR

The very first text of Jacques Prévert's 1946 *Paroles (Words)*, "Tentative de description d'un dîner de têtes à Paris-France" ("Attempt to Describe a Dinner of Heads in Paris-France", 1,3-12),[1] is enough, almost, to deter any effort to place his work in the context of the modern literary developments that precede it. This is a longish poem – but also a piece of prose – that, written in 1931, when Prévert was thirty-one years old, seems immediately to establish its own space, its own tone, its relative indifference to traditions whether Romantic or Symbolist, *esprit nouveau* or, in many respects, even Surrealist. As in the epigraph above, taken from "Le Cancre" ("The Dunce", 1,43), also of *Paroles*, Prévert's text seems to wipe the slate clean: the "traps" and constraints of language and history are pushed aside, the jubilation of the moment, Prévert's own moment of writing and riotous (self-) liberation, seems to be practically all that matters, the dance of words recounting the procession to the dinner party *is, now*, with no glancing back over the shoulder to Lamartine or Baudelaire, Mallarmé or even Apollinaire:

> Ceux qui pieusement...
> Ceux qui copieusement...
> Ceux qui tricolorent...
> Ceux qui inaugurent...

---

[1] All such references are to the two-volume Pléiade edition of Arnaud Laster and Danièle Gasiglia-Laster. All the translations are my own.

Ceux qui croient
Ceux qui croient croire
Ceux qui croa-croa
Ceux qui ont des plumes
Ceux qui grignotent
Ceux qui andromaquent
Ceux qui dreadnoughtent
Ceux qui majusculent
Ceux qui chantent en mesure
Ceux qui brossent à reluire
Ceux qui ont du ventre
Ceux qui baissent les yeux
Ceux qui savent découper le poulet
Ceux qui sont chauves à l'intérieur de la tête
Ceux qui bénissent les meutes
Ceux qui font les honneurs du pied
Ceux qui debout les morts
Ceux qui baïonnette... on
Ceux qui donnent des canons aux enfants
Ceux qui donnent des enfants aux canons
Ceux qui flottent et ne sombrent pas
Ceux qui ne prennent pas le Pirée pour un homme
Ceux que leurs ailes de géants empêchent de voler
Ceux qui plantent en rêve des tessons de bouteille sur la
    grande muraille de Chine
Ceux qui mettent un loup sur leur visage quand ils mangent
    du mouton
Ceux qui volent des oeufs et qui n'osent pas les faire cuire
Ceux qui ont quatre mille huit cent dix mètres de Mont
    Blanc, trois cents de Tour Eiffel, vingt-cinq centimètres
    de tour de poitrine et qui en sont fiers
Ceux qui mamellent de la France
Ceux qui courent, volent et nous vengent, tous ceux-là, et
    beaucoup d'autres entraient fièrement à l'Élysée en
    faisant craquer les graviers, tous ceux-là se bousculaient,
    se dépêchaient, car il y avait un grand dîner de têtes et
    chacun s'était fait celle qu'il voulait.
(Those who piously...
Those who copiously...
Those who flag-fly...
Those who inaugurate...
Those who believe
Those who believe they believe

8

Those who cro-croak
Those with feathers
Those who nibble
Those who andromache
Those who dreadnought
Those who capitalize
Those who sing in rhythm
Those who polish-brush
Those with a belly
Those who look away
Those who can carve chicken
Those who are bald inside their heads
Those who give blessing to mobs
Those who bring home the honors of the hunt
Those who rise up the dead
Those who with fi... bayonets
Those who give guns to children
Those who give children to guns
Those who float and don't sink
Those who don't think Queen Anne isn't dead
Those who can't fly because of their giants' wings
Those who in their dreams place broken glass on the Great
   Wall of China
Those who put a wolf over their faces when eating lamb
Those who steal eggs and don't dare cook them
Those who are fifteen thousand seven-hundred and seventy-
   one Mont Blanc feet, nine hundred and eighty-four Eiffel
   Tower feet, ten inches around the chest and proud of it
Those who give tits to France
Those who race and fly about, avenging us, all those and
   many more were proudly entering the President's Palace,
   crunching the gravel, all of them jostling one another,
   hurrying along, for there was a great dinner of heads and
   everyone had screwed on the one he wanted.)

The anaphoric cascade of words is irresistible, contagious, witty, full
of yet pertinent both general and specific allusions to social mores,
punning, satirical, freely flowing – and it is only the beginning of a
poem-cum-prose that will ceaselessly, implacably, affirm a literary
mode and human consciousness unique in the history of French
literature.

A uniqueness with affinities, of course: I'll have occasion to return to this. And, in fairness to my original project in this chapter, a uniqueness perhaps only fully appreciated if we take account of much that Prévert's work *isn't* or echoes only in parodical, spectral or significantly transmuted form. Indeed, Prévert's literary inheritance may arguably better be found in leaping beyond the century of Hugo and Balzac and Rimbaud, all the way back to Rabelais and even Villon. This has been the argument of critics such as Armand Hoog or Pascal Pia, whilst others, for example Gaëtan Picon, have looked closer to home in speaking of the pertinence of the work of Voltaire or Chamfort. In negative or contrastive terms Prévert has, too, of course, various allusions to La Fontaine and, most particularly, Pascal. Yet the nineteenth century drew his attention commonly, for better or for worse, and the names of Hugo, Zola, Lautréamont, Van Gogh and Rodin are readily observable, as is a spontaneously witty but ever meaningful intertextuality via which poets such as Vigny and Baudelaire may be flashingly evoked.

If we go back to the Romantic period, with Chateaubriand, Madame de Sévigny and its great poets from Marceline Desbordes-Valmore and Lamartine to Vigny and the early Hugo, there is much that has disappeared by the time the texts of *Paroles* are being written. Gone the sentimentalism. Gone the "new" heroism of Chatterton, Hernani, Jocelyn. Gone the dignity and dark, anxious glory of melancholy, suffering, exile. Gone untrammelled introspection. Gone the embrace of, even the struggle with, the divine of any vaguely Christian character. Gone, too, the fascination with formal and tonal constraints from which only partial liberation is sought by the Romantics. And yet, *toutes proportions gardées*, the heart rather than the head – it is no accident that the first poem of *Paroles* is a rich farce-cum-satire of Parisian heads – dominates Prévert's poetics; the individual's life is prized above any collective social structuring; love is an all-consuming preoccupation with Prévert; "nature" and a larger planetary even cosmic picture draw Prévert's attention in profoundly significant ways.

The great Realist novelists – Balzac, Flaubert, no doubt also Stendhal in various respects – are not writers Prévert speaks of particularly, nor does he allude to the work of the outstanding French Realist painters of the first part of the nineteenth century, such as Courbet, Millet, Daumier. This notwithstanding, the broad perspective in which their work unfolds clearly has some pertinence to the writing of a man for whom the real and a clear-eyed sense of its complex social, political, economic and psychological "truths" remain of central concern. Certainly Prévert is not inclined to create universalizing or overly generalized categories or structures, and he avoids the temptations of overarching orchestrations that might gather his "graffiti" into some *oeuvre* à la Balzac, à la Zola. Lexical *justesse*, yes, but anything approaching method or "science", no. Reasoned perception and organization has its limits for Prévert, although irony and quick-witted persiflage could only delight him and produce "wilder", sharper truth. The Realist's focus on the ordinary, its neglected relevance, depth and even beauty, ironised though they might be, are equally factors to be discovered in tonally modified form in Prévert, for apparently simple presence or occurrence always constitute for him deep sources of the extraordinary, the magical even – or, of course, of the extraordinarily ludicrous in human behavioral terms: "A Dinner of Heads" is a classic example here. Ultimately, the Realists refocus attention away from the mythical, the idealized, the aestheticized, and thus privilege life, daily, largely contemporary life in a way to which Prévert could not but be sensitive, even sympathetic.

The 1860-1890's work, on the other hand, of poets and painters of what we today largely deem to be Symbolist orientation – Baudelaire at least in part, Mallarmé, Rimbaud, Verlaine, Redon, Moreau, let us say – appears to be broadly predicated on a poetics not guaranteed to coincide with the needs, aspirations and impulses of the young, working-class Prévert. Not Prévert's the Mallarméan flight from fleshy, material existence. Not his the inclination towards the hermetic, the esoteric, the pursuit of a Beauty available via Baudelaire's dream of order and calmness – that Prévert parodies in "Anabiose"("Anabiosis"), from the 1966 *Fatras (Hodgepodge)*: "All is wounds and humps, hearses and gas-lamps, flirting, scalping, all-in-wrestling, voluptuousness"(2, 95) – or in Mallarmé's "absent flower of all bouquets", in the pure intellection of the poem's "minute monument to the soul". It is true that Verlaine's late witty, bawdy, compassionate poems to two aging prostitutes who showed him great kindness in his near-destitution would have pleased Prévert; that Rimbaud's provocations, his cutting lucidity and imperious "return", after his great bouts of *voyance*, to "rough reality", correspond to

11

essential impulses in Prévert; that a painter such as a Redon plumbs those depths of the psyche that the Surrealists will equally seek to explore. But hesitations, distinct differences remain: the persistence of religious symbols and constraints, principally, the frequent nostalgia for a "transcendence", as Baudelaire put it "anywhere out of the world", and a consequent incapacity to maintain quotidian joy and a buoyancy of earthy experience.

What, then, of a considerable gaggle of other, widely divergent genial talents of the last quarter of the nineteenth century – and let us not forget that Prévert's birth "backs" right up to such a period of fervent creativity: 4th February, 1900? What, then, of Zola, of Lautréamont, Laforgue, the Impressionists, Rodin, the budding Jarry? Naturalism's fatalistic, determinist bent would reduce Prévert's essential feeling of ever available personal (self-)empowerment, great as he viewed Zola's *Nana* and movingly true as he may have felt his social portrayals of social mores to have been. To the author of *Les Chants de Maldoror (The Songs of Maldoror)* is dedicated Prévert's "Opéra tonique" ("Tonic Opera") from the 1963 *Histoires et autres histoires (Stories and Other Stories)* and Prévert's quasi-autobiographical conversations with André Pozner, published in 1972, five years before his death, bear continued reference to this fiercely if depressively deconstructive prose poet, claimed as a precursor by Breton and other Surrealists for his "work of destructive irony" as Blanchot rather tendentiously writes. Laforgue's "decadent" fin-de-siècle *Complaintes (Dirges)* clearly find their echo in various texts of Prévert and the author of *Paroles* would have undoubtedly appreciated Laforgue's great wit, his ironic free-verse anti-poems, his honest (self-)mocking portrayals of psyche and society, metaphysical and philosophical elucubration, his undying impulse, too, towards love in its simplest, truest of forms. The Impressionists Prévert never mentions, in fact – the only Renoir he speaks of is the great early film-maker, with whom Prévert collaborated in the production of *Le Crime de Monsieur Lange (The Crime of Mr. Lange)*. But, if Degas and Manet might have been at times too bourgeois for Prévert's taste, he surely will have admired the former's often underrated attention to ephemeralness and anonymous human presence, and may well have appreciated the scathing pronouncements of the painter Frank Elgar called "this proud and merciless observer, this steadfast naturalist"; and as for Manet, the plain audacities of "Olympia" or "Déjeuner sur l'herbe" ("Luncheon on the Grass"), along with those portrayals that appealed equally to Renoir of gatherings and activities of ordinary people, could only delight a Prévert ever delighted by simple popular *fêtes* and fairs. And, of course, the fascination with the mystery and magic of light and color, texture and shape, of artists as different as Monet and Pissarro, Sisley and Cézanne, would largely feed into the passionate love for the multitudinous things of an earth Prévert felt increasingly to be ecologically challenged, even threatened. I shall have occasion later to allude to the admiration Prévert expresses for the work of Van Gogh, and similar feelings towards Rodin's art were no doubt fuelled by his ongoing mocking of Claudel's pronouncements on religion and his yet understandable antagonism, as his sister Camille declined into madness, towards the man behind the sculptor. As for Jarry and his impact on Prévert, finally, it would be difficult to overrate their pertinence: Jarry is a frequent reference point in the 1972 *Hebdromadaires (Weekly Camel Runs)*, where Prévert describes Breton's tears of laughter in reading the author of *Ubu roi (King Ubu)*; Prévert was, with Boris Vian and others, to belong to the virtual College of Pataphysics imagined by Jarry, and created his Terrace of the Three Satraps when, in 1955, he and his wife shared a terrace with Vian – the three "satraps" being Vian, Prévert and his dog Ergé: the "Lettre au Baron Mollet" ("Letter to Baron Mollet") is a riotously funny spoof à la Jarry (2,816-19), signed Jacques Pervers.

Much that is in Jarry's work may be said to correspond in spirit with the activities and writings of the young Dadaists and there is little doubt that their influence upon the equally young Prévert, seventeen at the time of Tzara's arrival in Paris, from Zurich, at Breton's invitation, would have been significant. However - we shall more fully explore this shortly - it was not until 1925 that Prévert was to meet Desnos and, through him, Péret and Aragon. Before long, Prévert knows Breton and is seeing the larger Surrealist group on a daily basis. If Dada's spirit of demolition, scandal and anarchical provocation persists, from 1924 on, with the publication of *Le Manifeste du surréalisme (The* [First] *Surrealist Manifesto)*, Surrealism has already begun to define its differences, those aspirations and growing expectations of an "absolute" that only existed implicitly in the jubilatory yet often anguished turmoil of Dada. This, to say that Prévert experiences Dada after the fact, in an already changed poetic and psychical climate. The declaration of war in 1914, however, plunges the adolescent Prévert out into the streets; his studies end; he works in little shops here and there, not always with entire legality uppermost in his mind; he is streetwise, getting by at best, sometimes at odds with the police; his elder brother dies of typhoid fever aged seventeen. If the First World War for many Dadaists represented a total collapse of all Western values, an exposure of the darker, at once material, psychological and visceral forces lurking within and catastrophically exploding the myths of human grandeur and intelligence, it cannot be said that Prévert emerged from the war with quite those sentiments and impulses. What Prévert himself tells us of his very early childhood explains in part why.

CHILDHOOD

In September and October of 1959, Prévert published in *Elle* magazine the bulk of an autobiographical sketch of the first ten or so years of his life in Paris and, briefly, Marseille and Toulon. "Enfance" ("Childhood", 2,215-53) was eventually taken up in 1972 as the opening text, in prose, of *Choses et autres (Of This and of That)*. What it reveals is critical to an appreciation of the broad cultural heritage of Prévert, a heritage perhaps subtly richer and more secretly determining in many respects that that we have just described, despite the latter's undoubted pertinence. Here are the opening paragraphs of this exquisite text of remembrance and celebration:

> 1906, Neuilly-sur-Seine
> Souvent, au Bois, un cerf traversait une allée. Un peu partout, les gens mangeaient, buvaient, prenaient le café. Un ivrogne passait et hurlait: «Dépêchez-vous! Mangez sur l'herbe, un jour ou l'autre, l'herbe mangera sur vous!»
> Le tramway du Val d'Or, à toute vapeur, sifflait le long des arbres, comme les trains dans les histoires d'Indiens. Le jour n'était pas encore éteint, mais déjà la Porte Maillot flambait, souhaitant la fête au crépuscule.
> Il y avait des cyclistes et des vélos, partout des vélos, encore des vélos et des voitures avec des chevaux.
> Ça sentait le caoutchouc et Bibendum régnait déjà sur le Salon de l'Automobile.

Au café des Sports, les garçons plantaient en courant deux pailles dorées dans la grenadine des enfants.

Cela sentait le Pernod, le crottin à oiseaux. Les arbres riaient et frissonnaient; rien encore ne les menaçait tout à fait.

Il y avait des gens qui faisaient la musique, qui chantaient, qui faisaient la fête, qui faisaient la gaieté, et ceux qui, à voix basse, s'engueulaient autour de leurs guéridons, étaient tout de même sous le charme et leurs injures, leurs pauvres menaces, on aurait dit qu'ils les chantaient, les fredonnaient sans y penser. Passaient des mendiants, des marchands d'olives, des musiciens ambulants et un vieux bonhomme qui remontait et posait sur les tables des jouets mécaniques.

(1906, Neuilly-upon-Seine.

Often, in the Bois de Boulogne, a stag would cross a walkway. More or less everywhere, people were eating, drinking, having coffee. A drunkard would go by and yell: "Hurry up! Eat on the grass, pretty soon the grass will be eating on you!"

The Val d'Or tram, under full steam, would whistle its way along the trees, like the trains in stories about Indians. The light wasn't yet faded, but already Porte Maillot was ablaze, giving festive wishes to the dusk.

There were cyclists and bikes, bikes everywhere, more bikes and carriages with horses.

Things smelled of rubber and the Michelin man already reigned over the Automobile show.

In the Café des Sports, the waiters would be racing about popping gold straws into the children's pomegranate cordials.

It smelled of absinth, bird droppings. The trees were full of laughter and all aquiver; nothing as yet really threatened them.

There were people making music, singing, carousing, having a merry time and those who muttered and argued away at each other around their tables still felt the spell upon them and it seemed as if they were singing their insults and weak threats – humming them away without much thought. Beggars would go by, olive-sellers, itinerant musicians and an old fellow who would wind up mechanical toys and put them on the tables.)

The dominant climate is one of teeming life, beyond the constraints of hierarchy. Intensity and ease join hands in a pre-war, childhood world of naturalness and innocence, festivity and shared magicalness. Human life seems couched and at home in a cosmos not at odds with anyone, and Prévert, both young and old, thrives on the multiplicity, the abundance, as well as the simplicity and the unpretentiousness of a great sensory and psychical theater in which his personal honoring seems a natural part of life's own celebration of its endless play.

"Enfance" ("Childhood") demonstrates, then, that what I have called the climate in which Prévert's entire *oeuvre* will come to unfold, is characterized by an instinctive and, in the twentieth century, rare openness to happiness, a collective and therefore individual sense of the mysterious enchantment available in our existence, a visceral and trusted personal knowledge of a rightness, an unproblematicalness, a strange but sure beauteousness lying deep within all things and all beings if we are able to give ourselves to them, maintain them, give assent and esteem to them despite the reservations and hesitations that can arise within us. Such a mental and psychological climate, "Enfance" repeatedly shows us, is a climate of attitude at once given and ceaselessly chosen, reasserted by Prévert, and it is largely beyond – although it corresponds to – literary and artistic criteria. Not that the young Prévert grew up at a distance from word and image. On the contrary, his mother had taught him how to read very young and he devoured Andersen, *The Arabian Nights* and popular adventure and serialized stories, sharing with his father pretty well anything either chose to read (cf. 2,251). As for images, Prévert's eyes, when not riveted on the rich kaleidoscope of raw yet fascinating and tenderly caressed scenes everywhere around him, turned not to the art stored in the museums and galleries of Paris, but rather to the popular theater, the flickering images of the earliest French cinema, the illustrations of ordinary magazines and largely cheap books.

Economics and social situation thus ruled and moulded this climate, yet, as with so many poor or working-class families, Prévert did not have to bear the burden of bourgeois constraints and demands and thus experienced a level of mental and physical freedom that undoubtedly shaped a psyche instinctively knowing the value, the beauty, the oddly privileged delight of such freedom. Not that Prévert felt neglected in any way; on the contrary, his family was close, loving, supportive, but in a spontaneous, unfussy way. His mother sang and laughed; his father regarded Prévert's mother as a magical fairy-like creature and didn't hesitate to tell his sons so, though they needed no convincing. True, there were moments, periods of great material difficulty and Prévert recalls the desperate depressiveness come upon his father not long after the birth of his younger brother, Pierre, with whom he was to collaborate in the production of many a film, and after the family's move to Marseille and then to Toulon in his father's urgent pursuit of work: the six-year old Jacques convinces his father to live and fight on as the latter is on the point of drowning himself as they roam together along the harbor front in Toulon. And the return to Paris within the year, whilst offering some financial improvement and job stability hardly brings about anything vaguely approaching modern comforts and luxuries, though Prévert insists – out of experience: he often accompanied his father in his new duties involving visits to the poor to determine what assistance might possibly be offered them – upon the staggeringly wretched slum conditions "enjoyed" by so many just after the turn of the century. "[N]ext to all that, our two rooms in Paris seemed like a palace" (2,248). If, Prévert's parents, moreover, were compassionate and antiracist – he affectionately remembers his father as saying there is nothing more foolish than joking about people's bodies: "When people are beautiful, they're beautiful, men or women, and from whatever country" (2,238) –, his grandfather, on the other hand, with his Catholic morality and sterner manner, often expressed his low view of "workers" (2,231) and a host of others: "women 'with their hair down', incendiaries, fops, tarts, fishwives, anarchists, sailors on a spree", all in the same category as site-workers, or worse. Views such as these, his relative disinclination towards schooling, his propensity to question and re-evaluate accepted norms – none of this seems to have shattered the spell childhood cast upon his sensibility and dawning consciousness. The sea at Pornichet, not far from La Baule, the long treks on holiday, the mimosas and eucalyptus trees of Les Sablettes or Tamaris on the Mediterranean, the vast, almost personal playground the Luxembourg gardens provided back in Paris from Toulon, the at least weekly family cinema outings with the noise-maker and his bells and hammers and revolver behind the screen, the romanies "always on the move, even when they're there", as Prévert's father would say, the American children he got to know young, with their "cowboy-artist father" – these and so many other intensely real experiences seem to have provided a framework in which there was no room for bitterness or indignation. The climate of enchanted, even if sometimes difficult, feasibility Prévert describes in 1959, and expands on in 1969, orients him rather towards the possibility of joy, (self-)transformation, festivity, the deployment of sheer swarming human energy in a world whose natural phenomena – flowers, waves, wind, trees – equally never cease to deploy their own abundant energy. "Enfance" shows clearly, however, that, if all this was felt, instinctively, by the young Prévert, sixty-odd years of life and largely adult experience have not dulled the original feelings. Prévert's writings, despite what various contemporaries argued,[1] are not at bottom refusals and antagonistic objections to much he observes in life: they ceaselessly choose rather to give assent to all that his own childhood showed him was always available: magic, freedom, love, joy – if, indeed, we truly want them and reaffirm their felt pertinence.

FINAL APPRENTICESHIPS

In March, 1920, Prévert is called upon to complete his military service which allows him to meet the future Surrealist painter Yves Tanguy, currently pretending to be mad and a spider-eater so as to be sent home; takes him to Istanbul where allied troops are on exercises; lands him in the "clinker" for his satirical remarks on the usefulness of colonels; gives him the difficult privilege of giving words of consolation to the mother of Roger, a young conscript-friend of Prévert's who commits suicide upon his return home and discovery of the infidelity of his equally young wife. To these preparatory experiences – war, freedom of speech, the beauty and difficulties of love's impulses will remain constant preoccupations of Prévert's oeuvre – are soon added those, in 1922, of working in a press agency, along with Yves Tanguy - from which they are both dismissed for fanciful exaggeration – and the discovery of Adrienne Monnier's soon to become celebrated bookstore. 1924 sees Prévert working as an extra down in Aix-en-Provence and his brother Pierre – soon to plunge into film production, often with Jacques' scripts, as

---

[1] Danièle Gasiglia-Laster and Arnaud Laster have scrupulously represented such views in their notes to the Pléiade edition.

we shall later see – already earning his living as a projectionist with Erko Prodisco. His marriage in 1925 to his childhood friend, Simone Dienne – a marriage lasting ten eventful years – coincides with a considerable expansion of his social and – for want of a better word (Prévert would, rightly, never cease to question its connotations and distorting applications) – "intellectual" horizons: meetings, and very soon discussions and actions of all kinds, with budding Surrealists and artists such as Desnos, Péret, Aragon, Breton and Giacometti. The two years that follow are filled with demonstrations, group and private exchanges and explorations often with a socio-political character and not just oriented towards what Breton termed "the real functioning of the mind", quarrels that can lead to Breton's "expulsion" of Artaud and Soupault, readings of work-in-progress, petitions connected with such things as Charlie Chaplin's love life or the erection of a monument to Rimbaud in his native town, further encounters with writers such as Raymond Queneau and Michel Leiris, and artists such as André Masson and Man Ray. (As Alain Rustenholz has argued, and as his numerous biographers-cum-critics show, Prévert's (hi)story is noticeably "collective" in many ways.)[1]

Such "apprenticeships" - of course, neither Surrealists nor Prévert believed much in programmes or ordered attachments and pursuits, despite their frequent, but usually strained dalliance with communism: freedom tended to be a *sine qua non* of life and work – such pseudo-apprenticeships, then, are angled away from exclusively aesthetic preoccupations and vastly exceed the traditional perspectives in which literature and artistic activity generally were contemplated. Values persist, and will always blossom and flower in Prévert's work – Michel Deguy could make much of this name, Green-Meadow, as he did, genially and appropriately, with the name of another great poet crucial to Prévert's period: Reverdy (:"Grown-green-again")[2] -, but these values are neither formal, symbolic, aesthetic, nor moral, ethical in conservatively, even logically codifiable terms. How are the "values" of psychic spontaneity, laughter, marvellous enigma to be rationally articulated and conceptually structured? How, even, are the tensions of unfettered dream and concrete social action to be smoothed out? These "apprenticeships" do not answer such questions,

---

[1] See selected Bibliography, as for other references to Prévert criticism.
[2] See Deguy's preface to the Gallimard collection Poésie edition of Reverdy's *Sources du vent/La Balle au bond*.

but they have the immense merit of *posing* them, of pushing the ever-maturing Prévert towards the complex consideration of our human options and possibilities, towards a growing comprehension of our and his liberty of choice, our and his very real, very free self-definability.

It is during the 1927-28 period that Prévert seems to have written the first of many scenarios to come, *Le Fils de famille (Family Son)*. The various scenarios of this period, often short, are intended for the nascent film world and, popular, witty, provocative, may or may not ever be used as intended. Moreover, via such work, Prévert slowly shifts his focus, attains heightened independence vis-à-vis the Surrealist group, so that, after already receiving from Breton a letter of "rupture" over a too-close-for-comfort prank connected with the elopement of Raymond Queneau and Janine Kahn (Breton's sister-in-law), 1930 finds Prévert, with others (Bataille, Carpentier, Desnos, Leiris, Vitrac, Queneau, etc.), rebelling against Breton's authoritarian leadership in the publication of a joint pamphlet to which Prévert contributes the short text "Mort d'un Monsieur" ("Death of a Gentleman"). That same year sees the production of cartoon scenarios of great bite and charm and film scripts such as *Attention au fakir (Watch out for the Fakir)*, which, along with his involvement in the two years that follow with the breakaway "revolutionary" theater group *Octobre*, definitively mark the moment when much of his early writing reaches a maturity permitting both ultimate literary recognition in *Paroles* and beyond, and, more immediately, a fully fledged career in the dynamic early film industry. Childhood literary inheritance and what I have termed Prévert's final apprenticeships give way to full-scale creativity, though, as I have argued, much that Prévert has "learned" never leaves him, even though its "lessons" never were nor ever will be stable for a mind intent on living the joy and the ever-questioning laughter of its freedom.

Je sais, un peu partout, tout le
monde s'entretue, c'est pas gai,
mais d'autres s'entrevivent, j'irai
les retrouver.
(I   know,   more   or   less
everyone is killing
everyone else, it's not that nice,
but others are living one another,
I'll go and join up with them.)
Jacques Prévert, *Fatras* (2,22)

SOCIAL STRUCTURES, IDEOLOGY

All of Prévert's work and the multifaceted perspectives on
social – and therefore, inevitably, philosophical and psychological –
mores it generates should be understood to hover between the
complementary poles of motivated, purposeful satire and the
liberating, detached, but equally purposeful gesture of laughter, sheer
life-affirming fun. The 1930 "Souvenirs de famille" ("Family
Reminiscences", 1,16-26), for example, from *Paroles* may expose
both the authoritarian mentality of many fathers and the authority
attributed to the ultimate Western father figure, "God the father, of
God Father Son Holy Ghost and Co.", but the sharp satirical
pertinence of such a text is equilibrated, both defused and oddly
intensified, no doubt, by the rampant wittiness everywhere on
display. Power, "greatness", politico-religious position, and the fears
and traumas they may develop in those exposed to them – "L'Effort
human" ("Human Effort", 1,63), also from *Paroles*, is a cascading
poem confirming the perils of "the head of the aggressive pacifier/the
policing head of the great liberator" – such factors can clearly have
bite and testy, testing incisiveness; but, almost invariably, either
Prévert's smile will break out or a vision of the feasible simplicity he
feels existence can attain to will somehow be articulated, at least
parenthetically. This is true even of "L'Effort humain", where the
image of man and wife and children, a few simple implements strung
across their shoulders, flashes before us: unreal, imaginable.
The religious beliefs, myths and doctrines that structure
societies – Prévert, understandably, centers his work upon Western

cultures and mores – are well known to enjoy special privileges at the center of Prévert's satire – that is, at the center of the *questions* he puts to our modern culture and the social structures it supports. The myth of the father whose power is inalienable derives and is solidly encouraged by patriarchal religions, Prévert "argues". The poem-scenario – generically, he loves to sow smiling dissension – Prévert gives us in "La Famille tuyau de poêle ou Une famille bien unie" ("The Stovepipe Family or A Well-Knit Family", 1,739-67) from the 1955 *Là Pluie et le beau temps (Rain and Shine)* offers a farcical and parodic portrayal of adultery, incest, secrecy, military mentality, empty exploitation of religious texts.

The problem that Prévert thus has with religion and its various dogmas is not, of course, that notions of love and charity are notionally at their root, but, on the contrary, that these highest principles can be so easily cast aside, complexing people, fostering guilt, shame, sense of separation, eschewing often natural ebullience, giving fixity to the joyous mystery of life via the imposition of interpretative grills, the favoring of certain texts (the Scriptures) over all others. It is because these structurings – penetrating profoundly the realms of male-female relations, father-family relations, education, nation state concepts and so on – lack all suppleness and openness, generating rather intolerance and severity, that Prévert can speak in "Graffiti", from *Choses et autres*, of "revolution [being] sometimes a dream, religion always a nightmare" (2,276); contrast on repeated occasions the rhetoric and at times outrageous absurdities in times of holy, mystical warfare and national interest not only of politicians and popes or archbishops but also writers such as Claudel and Péguy or Teilhard de Chardin, with the clear-mindedness of a Lorca or a Blake (cf. "Les Règles de la guerre" ("The Rules of War", 2,22-32)); write tongue-in-cheek poems such as "Écritures saintes" ("Holy Scriptures", 1,112-15) or transform the notion of Holy Face into that of Holy Farce (cf. "La Transcendance" ("Transcendence", 1,236). Let it be stressed, these deflations and deconstructions are not designed by Prévert to hurt or to offend: they almost always emanate from quoted material, from that mass of press clippings Prévert kept in endless dossiers, and they seek to encourage free thinking, as well as inoffensive fun in the midst of highly provocative and influential social myths that form / deform us – with, or course, our acquiescence.

Prévert's witty and entirely appropriate questioning of the psychology and methodology of teaching, in "Pourquoi pourquoi" ("Why Why", 2,56-7) from *Fatras* gives us the delightful truth:

> Il n'y a pas de problème
> Il n'y a que les professeurs
> (There isn't any problem
> There are only professors);

for, indeed, life – and surely we can reasonably follow Prévert here – *is* unproblematic in an intrinsic way and only becomes cluttered the more we lay on it *our* limitations, *our* assumptions, *our* psychologico-philosophico-sociological form. It is for this reason that Prévert dislikes the very ideas of "lesson" and "knowledge" the way we usually imagine them – I'll come back to this, shortly. And it is for this reason that – again, as we shall shortly see somewhat better – the very idea of a Prévertian ethics or even counter-ethics remains a very tricky and prickly issue. Pragmatists may feel Prévert can thus escape with satirical blue murder. But he still remains difficult to fault in his implacable exposure – but an exposure still buoyant, laughingly inviting of commonsensical adjustment – of our socially and psychologically flawed conception and practice of, say, economics. "Le Discours sur la paix" ("Peace Speech", 1,141), from *Paroles*, surely rings many a contemporary bell:

> Vers la fin d'un discours extrêmement important
> le grand homme d'État trébuchant
> sur une belle phrase creuse
> tombe dedans
> et désemparé la bouche grande-ouverte
> haletant
> montre les dents
> et la carie dentaire de ses pacifiques raisonnements
> met à vif le nerf de la guerre
> la délicate question d'argent.
> (Towards the end of an extremely important speech
> the great Statesman stumbling
> over a lovely hollow sentence
> falls in
> and all at sea and mouth agape
> panting away

bares his teeth
and the dental decay of his pacific arguments
exposes the nerve of war
the delicate matter of money.)

Reasonable social mores may seem to dictate a logic of cooperation and peace – unless the economics of war turns out to be more profitable. "Bruits de coulisse" ("Offstage Noises",1,223-34) marshals a slew of quotations which show that the principle of social harmony and decency can be quickly sacrificed to monetary interest: exploitation may reign, state and church now led by, now leading, industry and business.

The delightful 1952 book, *Lettre des Îles Baladar (Letter from the Baladar Islands,* 1,523-54), illustrated by André François is the wittiest parody of colonial machinations where military and economic interests would seek to override all psychological, ecological and truly spiritual considerations in the social contract. For Prévert, worthy social structures would, implicitly, be non-interfering, naturally utopian, in tune with the natural rhythms of seasons and honest, innocent human impulses. The militarism of Western colonialism and neo-colonialism that so many of Prévert's texts deconstruct, partly in mocking disbelief, partly via vigorous satire, runs utterly contrary to such natural and simple deployment of energy. "There is no good or bad war" Prévert reaffirms in *Hebdromadaires* (2,880-81), still utterly disregarding of the criticism levelled at him for such attitudes during the Second World War. He will not hesitate to echo the views of many ordinary Americans in his dismayed condemnation of "the horrible, frightful, sordid fighting waged by the Pentagon gang against the Vietcong"(2,899). The nobility, the simple human decency of our social mores crumble away, he feels, as napalm burns man, woman and child (cf. "Entendez-vous gens du Vietnam..." ("Do You Hear People of Vietnam...", 1,651-7)), as modern weaponry "industrializ[es] death", as arms production proliferates, turning our civilization into "a civilization of waste, and first and foremost human waste" (cf. 2,883,888,928). And if the answer we might give to Prévert's question, "Will we die of hunger if we stop making deadly war machines?", is a guarded "No, but ...", then what does that tell us of the ideology underpinning our so-called peace-loving, peace-making cultures?

Criticize as we may Prévert's stance on our modern social psychology, it is hard to resist his explicit and implicit contention that what he calls, in "Un beau jour" ("One Fine Day...") from *Spectacles* (1,360), the all-too-frequent union of nations via "the sacred bonds of slaughter" also fuels the fires of an excessive patriotism that in turn, emphasizes difference, feeds the world's xenophobias, desensitizes us all to mass murder and the win-at-all-costs tactics or simple "side-effects" of war (ideally waged, as Prévert points out, "elsewhere"): torture, starvation, deprivation, prostitution and so on. All colonial powers and all neo-imperialist superpowers have been there, and Prévert never, *never* spares the French, "world champions" for years, he typically can assert, in various of these categories, all naturally involving "the exploitation and exporting of the Marseillaise" - the National Anthem (cf. 1,653). All of this, of course, depends upon a learned and constantly reaffirmed process of perception, of self and of other; upon a long-matured, but for Prévert decaying, rotten, set of assumptions about self and other, about ends and means, about the relativity of freedom and the acceptability of constraint, force, policing, etc. - about, too, the inevitability of fear (and therefore aggressive "self-defence") and the unreality, the impracticality of (unconditional) love and unjudging compassion. Ideology, in a word, and the psychological tension that holds ideology in place. Ideology is revealed, no doubt in Prévert's view, by the dominant action or inaction, voice or silence of a society. Poems such as "La Majorité silencieuse" ("The Silent Majority") or "Le Pouvoir" ("Power") (2,823-4) can, now sympathetically, now provocatively, test the reader's nerve on ideological issues and Prévert is in no doubt as to our *slavery* (cf. *Hebdromadaires* (2,908) to ideas and concepts that, for some reason, we feel the need to attach ourselves to, define our identity by, unfree ourselves by. Ideology, for Prévert, is quite simply the opposite of freedom. No "lock-step" for him, just as there is none for young children he argues, no "Stalin superstar" thinking, no "Jesus-Christ superstar" thinking (cf. *Hebdromadaires* (2,864,908). Children, like Prévert himself, see no need - unless it is hammered into them, subtly or otherwise - to cling to any ideological absolute, what Prévert can call a "God", whether "Marxist, Freudian, New-Look, Goncourt Prize or Knight of Academic Napalm" (*Fatras*, 2,21).

ANARCHY, FREEDOM

Is, then, Prévert an anarchist, as some have accused him of being? (Arnaud Laster and Danièle Gasiglia-Laster meticulously record the hyper-conservative outcry.). Certainly not, I shall maintain, if anarchy implies mental and emotional drift leading to acceptance of the social, planetary status quo, and a deteriorating status quo at that: Prévert's work is combative, as Claude Roy asserts, resistant, centered on exposure and a reminder of our fundamental existential options. There is nothing "indifferent" - despite what he may occasionally say about himself - or fatalistic in Prévert. A poem such as "Chanson des sardinières" ("Song of the Sardine Girls"), from *Spectacle* (1,332-3), may begin and end with the refrain,

Tournez tournez
petites filles
tournez autour des fabriques
bientôt vous serez dedans
tournez tournez
filles des pêcheurs
filles des paysans
(Dance around dance
little girls
dance around the factories
soon you'll be inside
dance around dance
fishermen's daughters
farmers' daughters,

but it remains a song of energy, youthful celebration, real and potentially symbolic "revolution", and not just a recognition of immutable social conditions. Nor is such dancing energy anarchic in any negative sense: it is part of that life-force which Prévert asks us never to neglect - and which is, once more, manifest in the gestures of children rather than the resigned acts of adults.

No, Prévert's anarchical tendencies are imbued with desire, dream, ideality; they are clarifying, non-abusive, angled towards vital simplicity, simple (self-)revitalisation. The native population depicted in the charming *Lettre des Îles Baladar* gives imaginative flesh to such simplicity and shows that anarchy may be lived as a festive, childlike embrace of truth, peacefulness, happiness. And the anonymous "individual" of the hallucinatory *Guignol (Punch and Judy)* Prévert publishes in 1952 with the fine illustrations of Elsa Henriquez - does he not implicitly *ask* "what if we did what we want in life?", even though he explicitly exclaims "if we did what we want in life!" (1,572). In effect, *Guignol* becomes the seemingly anarchical story of a reluctant, but non-abusive and benevolent redistribution or sharing of wealth. Its "anarchy", as with other poems - "Soyez polis" ("Be Polite", 1,822-4), from *Histoires et autres histoires* comes to mind - involves witty, fanciful inversions, transformations and pirouettes, purposeful and fun-loving simultaneously, transformations moreover that prize our grip off cherished concepts and prejudices and edge us towards that strange zone of non-possession, non-attachment, non-belonging - a zone not of having, but of *being* and *pure* love of life. We can call it anarchy if we like, but at least, smilingly, let us call it New Anarchy!

Judging by the words of the nightwatchman in "La Crosse en l'air" ("Sticks Up", from *Paroles* - but, then, is every character of Flaubert's novels, despite his words concerning Madame Bovary, absolutely assimilable to its author? - Prévert's atheism is pretty solidly anchored and is an instinct, rather than a belief, one can but respect. As he says with characteristic gusto in the poem of the same title, "I've always been intact from God" (2,254). But Prévert's *a*theism, like his so-called *anti*clericalism (which he disputes as a notion) or his *anti*totalitarianism or his *anti*intellectualism - all of these stances are neither fixed, absolute, nor bloody-minded, wilfully destructive. His "new anarchy" is not the behaviour of a literary hooligan any more than it is that of a flighty seeker of the limelight. Prévert's anticlericalism is the response of a human being unable to keep quiet about the severity and psychological traumatizing dogma can inflict upon many. His refusal of so-called patriotic "duty", of "rules", of imposed "lesson" (cf. "Sur le champ" ("On the Spot", 1,345), from *Spectacle)* stems, honorably, from his observation of the contradictoriness, not to say the hypocrisy, inherent in the social mores we have already outlined. The dangers of not questioning - albeit buoyantly, with vigorous exhilaration: otherwise, depression and demoralisation are around the corner - are concisely mapped out in "Futuralisme" ("Futuralism", 2,315) from *Choses et autres*:

> Dans les corridors suburbains de la Supercité, les agents de l'Intelligence publique demanderont aux passants, s'il en reste, leurs «idées», leur permis d'idéologie surveillée et, dans la plupart des cas, leur « uit » (unique idée tolérée).
>
> Ceux qui ne seront pas en règle seront appréhendés et dirigés vers le bloc opératoire culturel et universel.
>
> L'élucubrator les conduira au greffe de la culpabilité collective et de la responsabilité dirigée.
>
> Là, les grands manipulateurs leur perforeront le ticket socio-cérébral et ils seront remis en liberté maniable, manoeuvrable et manutentionnée.
>
> (In the suburban corridors of the Supercity, Public Intelligence agents will ask passers-by, if there are any left, for their "ideas", their supervised ideology licence and, in most cases, their "oti" (one tolerated idea).
>
> Those who aren't in order, will be arrested and sent to the cultural and universal operating unit.
>
> The Elucubrator will take them to the Office of the Clerk of the Court for Collective Guilt and Directed Responsibility.
>
> There, the great manipulators will punch their socio-cerebral ticket and they will receive their adjustable, manoeuvrable and manhandled freedom.)

Not a pretty picture, although amusing and parodical - though, yet again, chillingly evocative of totalitarian excesses seen and still visible around our globe. A witty warning, in short, not to be ruled by state, ideology, educators, by anything other than one's love and respect for freedom and honest difference. If any lesson emerges from Prévert's work, writes Yvan Audouard, it is freedom's refusal of hypocrisy.

"Le Droit Chemin" ("The Straight and Narrow", 1,108), from *Paroles,* leaves us in no doubt as to Prévert's sense of the potential and all too frequent loss of our glorious native spontaneity and freedom of option:

> À chaque kilomètre
> chaque année
> des vieillards au front borné
> indiquent aux enfants la route
> d'un geste de ciment armé
> (At each mile
> each year

old narrow-minded men
show children the way
with a wave of their concrete arms.)

"Anarchy" demands the right to natural suppleness, self-discovery, self-definition and self-possession. "Mustn't let ourselves be owned", is the cry of the workers of "Marche ou crève" ("Keep Moving or Die"), from *Spectacle* (1,328). The "wild" self-determination of Prévert's "first donkeys", in his sparkling 1947 *Contes pour enfants pas sages (Tales for Misbehaving Children*, 1,872), is the ideal, utopian - possible - behaviour. It can provide a life beyond flags, difference (of color, nationality, fortune, etc.), as Prévert strenuously argues in his tribute to the artist Gérard Fromanger, "Rouge" ("Red", 2,353-63). Beyond all ideas: life's freedom, in its purest state. Indeed, it was the limitation André Breton inclined to place upon the latter - ironically, for such freedom remained dear to Breton's heart, of course - that was at the center of Prévert's quarrel with him in 1930 (cf. 2,836). The opening poem of *Lumières d'homme (Lights of Man*, 1,632), of the same title concludes by asking, or rather affirming, for the question is rhetorical:

> qu'est-ce que ça fout pourvu que ça flambe.
> (What does it bloody matter as long as it flames away.)

This is not the fire of revolution or destructive indifference that Prévert preaches. But the freedom of love, its light, its warmth. A freedom beyond the constraints of state, church, doctrine and ideology of any kind; the same freedom he claims for Angela Davis (cf. 2,348-50), for the Rosenbergs (cf. 2,812), for all women - "misogyny mother of wars", he exclaims in *La Pluie et le beau temps* (1,660) - for all men, all children. A freedom that demands respect for the self, respect for the other, laughingly, warmly, naturally.

LANGUAGE, INTELLIGENCE, SCIENCE

The full extent of Prévert's linguistic play will be assessed in a later chapter. Suffice it to say here that, always, such play demonstrates a will to deconstruct the appropriations and seeming fixities of language's semantic and symbolic structures and equations. The fact that, as we have already seen, a god-like truth can attach itself to the language, the jargon, of almost any well-propagated idea, whether "Marxist, Freudian, New-Look, Goncourt Prize, Knight of Academic Napalm" (2,21), only pushes Prévert towards a finer, more ludic conception and manipulation of language, whose power, whose potentially absolute power, he clearly deems a dangerous intoxication to which we so easily succumb - and aggressively, addictively cling: the language of the world's countless isms. Towards the end of his spontaneous "interviews" with André Pozner, Prévert openly speaks of "the vocabulary of people, especially well brought up people, educated people, very cultured people, [which] is more and more war-like and religious"(2,899). Language becomes belligerent, fanatical, a means of obtaining and maintaining power, rather than a means of questioning, opening, freeing.

As early as *Paroles* (1,140), Prévert had, of course, affirmed, playfully and seriously as ever:

> Le monde mental
> Ment
> Monumentalement.
> (The mental world
> Is a monument of
> Lies.)

A poem such as this ("Il ne faut pas" ("We mustn't")) lays the groundwork for many others to come, where a fundamental scepticism as to the (mis)uses to which we can put our human intelligence is expressed. Intellection builds systems, intellectual monuments, artificial creations that can blind us to their relativity, their perhaps initially innocent "lie"- but one so easily turned abusive, authoritarian, one whose purely experimental status is forgotten because of the prestige or power it bestows. The posthumously published bit of Prévertian graffiti, "De la mort aux rats à la mort aux hommes" ("From Death to Rats to Death to Men", 2,927), evokes this slippage in very French terms:

> Fantômas se vantait de ses crimes,
> Savantas, lui, leur trouve des excuses.
> (Fantômas boasted of his crimes, whereas
> Savantas finds excuses for them.)

Whereas Fantômas - fictional antihero of the prewar popular literary and film world of Prévert's childhood and youth - is straightforwardly recognized for what he is, an all-powerful criminal rogue, Savantas is modern man justifying and rationalizing everything and anything that suits his often dubious ends by misapplying language, knowledge, intelligence. Seen in this light, it is not surprising that with typical flair, Prévert can say, of intelligence, in "La Sagesse ou les poux dans la tête" ("Wisdom or Lice on the Head", 2,943), "it's a sickness, a virus, and the intelligentsia [is] the secret society of the people most afflicted".

In the eyes of Prévert, the purely rational and rationalizing, and consequently self-interested pursuit of knowledge affects negatively science and business, government and the individual. So much is *omitted*, wittingly, or unwittingly, in such a pursuit. In a delightful letter-poem from the 1970 *Imaginaires (Imaginaries)*, which he signs "Someone Escaped from the Future", Prévert, addressing the "supermen" of the age, writes: "I wish you much enjoyment, you'll have so much to do, except love, dream, or raise your glass to the beauty of women, the health of friendship" ("Correspondance"("Correspondence", 2,170)). Young people, Prévert happily feels, always pierce through the stultifications and insensitivities of "science" in all its formalizing and dehumanizing modes. "They don't want to know anything about your knowing", he declares in "Des jeunes..." ("The Young...", 2,439). And yet the young are vulnerable. He quotes Montaigne while speaking with Pozner: "And how many men have I seen in my time, made stupid by rash greed for knowledge!" (cf. 2,879). The pursuit and formalization of knowledge may disfigure, abort and stifle truth's greater simplicities - and mysterious depths. "And those who stifle [truth]", he continues to tell Pozner in *Hebdromadaires* (2,906), "are said to be fountains of knowledge".

This *dis*figuration, this *de*magicking of the real, as Prévert sees it (cf. 2,907), may imply conscious perversion, conscious abuse, or it may be the result of Montaigne's observed stultification, a blinding of the self, and others, to the naturally intuited or experienced. Modern progress, industrial, technological, *may* have its material and other benefits. But "progress" for Prévert remains largely a movement taking us, as he says in *Arbres (Trees)*, nowhere everywhere, and fast (cf. 2,155). He speaks, in *Choses et autres*, of a lone voice crying out, not "forward, forward", but, funnily, "Backward!" It was, he writes - and this clearly is not Prévert's nostalgia, but simply his resistance to the blind movement of the pack - "a child's voice, the wild and joyful voice of one of time's outlaws" (2,309). To step *back* from the rationalizations of progress allows us to realize to what extent colonial, economic, industrial "progress" has often depended and still depends so often on exploitation, "extermination" even (cf. 2,980), at best difference so as to better benefit therefrom. The agendas of science and rationalizing intelligence, abetted by language's appropriations and expropriations, provide a "progress [that is] a legless cripple, but one making giant strides"("Rouge"("Red", 2,357)). A progress of the heart, of the sensibility, as we shall soon see, rather than of the head and the pocket in which the head sits, is what Prévert implicitly favors.

CHILDREN, PEOPLE

The eye of the child, Prévert can constantly argue, perceives much that we risk losing in this increasingly blind and forgetful forward rush we can term progress, success, control, "scientific" systematization and rationalization. The child's mind, equally, seeks freshness, new imagination, spontaneity. His or her heart thrives on love, the simple happiness of body, mind and spirit. All of Prévert's many poems and books for children - *Le Petit Lion (The Lion Cub), Des bêtes... (Of Animals...), Lettre des Îles Baladar (Letter from the Baladar Islands), Guignol (Punch and Judy), L'Opéra de la lune (Moon Opera)* and so on - appeal to a child's sense of humor, natural justice and wisdom, his or her slightly wild and mischievous fervor, a feel for the charm and magic of a truly possible innocent world. "L'Enfant abandonné" ("The Abandoned Child", 1,295-8), from *Spectacle*, gives wonderful insight into the imaginative ingenuity and emotional resilience that are the heritage, Prévert clearly feels, of all children: "incomprehensible dirges" sung to the self, "invented words [climbing all over one another]", "forbidden words, sacred and suddenly funny words, stolen words, pidgin, naked talk picked up in the streets", dreaming laughter. And, as Prévert so splendidly writes - for these are the teeming street children of early twentieth-century Paris, children today to be found all over the world - "well bred adults, at the sight of these little carnivores, run away uttering the sinister and puerile cry of the vegetarian lost in the abattoirs and this scream makes the children laugh and this scream gives them pleasure, truly" (1, 298).

Prévert, it is reasonable to say, may give a kind of "preference" to poor, deprived, working-class children, but this is no doubt because, as with the above "abandoned child" and the little "carnivorous" brothers and sisters met in the street, in lacking the coddling constraints and channellings imposed by middle-class parents living for and even *through* their offspring, they attain to a freedom, a naturalness, a spontaneity of discovery and expression that Prévert felt, having experienced them himself, to be in touch with our life-force, our primordial human energy. That children, whether poor or rich, can be abused, exploited, "hunted" (cf. "Chasse à l'enfant" ("Child Hunt", 1,57)), shackled, predetermined (cf. 1,295), exposed to the conscious or unconscious "disfigurations" and "demagickings" (cf. 2,907) of adults, Prévert is only too aware. "L'Enfant de mon vivant" ("The Child of my Lifetime"), from *La Pluie et le beau temps,* portrays a child - that Prévert was and still is - with his "sun-filled lunar song / his vulgar song envied and scorned / his down-to-earth starry / song" (1,787), a child who swears never to be "their man / since their man is a thinking reed", a child free as the wind, smiling, dancing off into the open, untold mystery of the world (cf. 1,788).

The social and ethical vision emblematized by such a child is not just predicated on revolt and resistance, though the latter may so frequently be required to avoid the fatal slippage into an "adult" mentality surprisingly so quick to jettison joy, innocence and imaginative and physical liberty. It is interesting, then, in this context, to see the undying affection Prévert vows to ordinary people, workers, those remote from and, as Prévert argues, commonly put down by both the intelligentsia (cf. "Bruits de coulisse" ("Offstage Noises", *Spectacle*, 1,225-7)) and "le Beau Monde" (cf. "Pour rire en société" ("Laughing in Society", 1,287)) - the world of the wealthy and powerful. Of course, as with the children Prévert depicts or addresses, these ordinary people are, in large measure, the inhabitants of his own early world: either the people he grew up with in a material context of fundamental adequacy, or those, terribly disadvantaged, that he visited with his father to assess for the city of Paris their relative wretchedness. "Aubervilliers" (1,335-7), a three-part poem from *Spectacle* put to music by Joseph Kosma and sung by Germaine Montero and Fabien Loris in the 1945-6 film produced by Eli Lotar, speaks with great intensity of both the appalling living conditions and great "simple dreams" of workers and children of this conurbation on the northern fringe of Paris. For Prévert, dreams are not synonymous with the pretentiousness of many intellectuals, and the cares and tribulations of ordinary people and the "gentle children of proletarians" (cf. 1,336) are not to be compared to the "biliousness" and viciousness of uppercrust society, *le Beau Monde* (cf. 1,287). Prévert respects and esteems the essentially magnanimous mind-set of those men and women who work and toil in our modern towns and cities: the 1951 *Grand Bal du printemps (Great Spring Ball)*, with Izis' wonderful photographs, gives us many a celebration of such "popular", bottom-of-the-Hugo-pyramid energy contributing to the construction of our collective social "masterpiece":

> Et anonymement généreusement largement
> ce chef-d'oeuvre chaque jour
> sa main-d'oeuvre le signe
> d'un grand paraphe de sueur de fatigue et de sang
> et de rires et de lueurs et d'amour du métier
> (And anonymously generously amply
> this masterpiece every day
> is signed by its labor force
> with a great flourish of sweat fatigue and blood
> and laughter and glimmerings and love of one's work.)

What this section of *Grand Bal du printemps*, *"À force de tirer..."* *("By Pulling..."*, 1,451-3), shows, is that not only is Prévert not a pure anarchist, nor a pure social cynic, but he even takes pride in the great strange creations we call our cities, he loves them whilst recognizing their problems and weaknesses - a reread of "Enfance" ("Childhood") or a viewing of his great film, made with Marcel Carné, *Les Enfants du paradis (The Children of Paradise)* will quickly convince us - , and he marvels at the astonishing mixture of joy and pain and love generating, driving on the construction of our collective social theater. And all of this vast deployment of human vigor and emotion occurs "anonymously": beyond the traps of high pride and creative hubris that Yves Bonnefoy has similarly warned against, as rather a simple insertion of ordinary people's "simple dreams" and sweat-stained gestures into the fabric of the ephemeral, the mortal - that fabric held together by ropes that break and which people patch up (cf. 1,452-3).

Nothing in the above should lead us to believe that Prévert idealized working-class living conditions or the mentality of ordinary people struggling to cope with them. He knew the profound disappointments and devastations that poverty, absolute or relative, can bring, the drab landscape of ordinary people's lives, "the landscape without air light laughter or seasons / the icy landscape of worker cities icy in midsummer", as he writes in "Le Paysage changeur" ("The Changing Landscape", 1,59-61) from *Paroles*. But just as Prévert knew that the buoyant, simple, surging energy of hard-working people everywhere, in America as in France, could be challenged to the point of tears and great suffering, so too did he know - the *same* poem finally swings round to show it - that the same people could dig deep into their resources, their will and desire for decency, joy and warmth, to "change winter into spring" (cf. 1,61), to operate personal, grassroots transformation of the landscape of their being. Prévert, let me emphasize, is not dealing here, or anywhere, with abstract, politico-philosophical change. "Man doesn't interest me", he confirms to André Pozner, "what interests me, what I love, are women, children, men" (*Hebdromadaires*, 2,870). People, raw life, not intellectualized banter. And from the year or so spent in the USA, Prévert remembers neither grand statesmen or writers any more than he dwells upon the racial or other contradictions of a few. What stays with him is, quite simply, the "love of the people I loved" (2,891). Something anonymous, unpretentious; something deeply personal, deeply essential. No wonder Clancier and Picon and others can see Prévert as "the most tender of elegiacal poets", the most soberly yet warmly "fraternal" of writers.

VALUES?

Given Prévert's sympathies for Lautréamont, Jarry, Dada and Surrealist impulses and given too that quasi-anarchical bent to much of his writing, it is not unreasonable, rather than to proceed immediately to list the values Prévert undoubtedly sees and seeks to see proliferate in life, to nevertheless pose the question of their feasibility, their status, their relation to all that many critics of Prévert regard as his scepticism, deconstructive vision, what he himself can term, as we have seen, a haunting "indifference" to existence. In brief, we may say the following: 1. Prévert is neither bloody-minded, gratuitously provocative, nor inclined to imagine the world in politically or philosophically transformable terms; 2. he is given neither to careless, thoughtless, unprincipled deconstruction, nor to the fabrication of new social constructs or "models", for he is not a preacher in socio-political terms nor a doer in an abstract way; 3. Prévert *does* have vision, social, "ethical", "spiritual" - in the broadest sense we can give to these terms - and certain ways of being *do count very much* for him, but he will not ruin his life *bemoaning* their frequent absence, moving rapidly instead from lucid exposure of problem to a celebration of such ways both in himself and in others living and acting by them.

Value, for Prévert, is never simply aesthetic, moreover, never at the surface, to do with form, structural relationships. Beauty remains a fundamental criterion, but not in the sense that he associates it particularly with literary or artistic creation and the latter as an act and a place of esoteric, hermetic retreat. Beauty must be a factor relating to basic existential experience: rather than a privileged, sheltered phenomenon fleeing life and isolated from it, the poem, the book, the painting, music should insert beauty into life, show us its general feasibility, its source in simple things and simple acts, its synonymity with love and natural embrace of life's strange, uncomplicated wonders. As Prévert says at the end of his marvellous 1950 text, *Des bêtes...*, accompanying and inspired by the equally marvellous photographs of Ylla, life, "when it is horrible and so to speak absurd and as you say unliveable troubling / it is never as horrible absurd unliveable troubling as it is beautiful when it's beautiful" (1,209). Beauty as an intrinsic quality and value at the center of life, despite all else... Beauty as that quality, that value within each of us, which, as the student Hamlet explains to his teacher, in "L'Accent grave" ("The Grave Accent", 1,40) from *Paroles*, allows us "to be where we may not be" - "être « où » ne pas être" -, to assume our being despite its possible existential challenge.

Value, then, for Prévert, is, as it were, embedded in being, synonymous with it, as mysterious and as simple as it. Value does not involve the reduction of the earth, our experience of the earth, to neat equations. Clearly we are incapable of this - "the earth looks at the earth", Prévert writes in *Imaginaires*, "everybody looks at everybody, nobody understands a thing" ("Terre à terre" ("Down to Earth", 2,190)) - and what is more, it is not what matters in Prévert's eyes. Openness, taking in the world, looking at it, living it beyond intellectual reduction and categorisation, remains a value of far greater import. And just as *being* in the midst of the temptations "not to be" has natural, intrinsic value - "ethical", visceral, emotional, "spiritual" value -, so, for Prévert, does *being* always take precedence over *having*, whether what is involved is things or people. Possession is never, for him, what can lead to value. As he says in "Graffiti" (2,275), from *Choses et autres*,

> Je ne veux pas t'avoir mais, comme je t'aime,
> je peux t'être
> (I don't want to have you but, as I love you,
> I can be you.)

Value accruing from the quality of (relations of) being, from relating in love to what, or who, is...

Such a perception of value, moreover, is intimately bound up with Prévert's sense of the central pertinence of both freedom and what he sees as the natural "wild", impulsive - but, as we have seen, non-abusive, non-exploitative - expression of our being. "Flags in vain flutter and float about like monetary values, like thousands of dead fish on filthy polluted rivers, or the wreckage of a trawler cut in two by a nuclear submarine", Prévert argues in "Rouge" ("Red", 2,362) in 1971, "the freest of the earth's children have no saint to devote themselves to, no worshipping to give or receive, no bit of tinsel to salute. // Only their freedom to defend, only their life to transform, only love to love". The value of freedom - and, let it be stressed, we are far from aesthetic, "arty" considerations only - merges with the value of life itself, just as the latter is not separable from the experience of love, can only maintain its value, its worth, if love suffuses life's time and space. To "tame" such freedom, as *they* - teachers, scientists, politicians, philosophers, sociologists, psychologists, etc., implicitly - might incline to do in imposing their conceptual structures on "wild children" ("Méningerie" ("Meningerie", 2,439)), is to risk stifling the values of openness, mystery, spontaneity, infinite feasibility of being which, only, truly count for Prévert. "Wild thought", as Prévert calls it in his conversations with André Pozner (2,909), may be recognized as having value by "learned thought", but it loses out to interest and power groups pushing "progress" and control. Value, for Prévert, lies in the honoring of the intrinsic virtue of wild, free-wheeling thought and being.

Such value is not predicated on foisting upon others the simplicities, the beauties, the truths obtainable by doing "what one likes", but recognizes the natural, commonsensical rightness of this latter tactic: "it's what I like that pleases me / and that I do" ("Malgré moi..." ("In Spite of Myself...", 2,255)). It is true, certainly, that affirming one's own values involves resistance and counter-attack; it is true that much needs to be "rendered less macabre" in our collective view of being (cf. "Intermède" ("Interlude", *Spectacle*, 1,377)), that to achieve a sense of those values Prévert cherishes much "dedramatizing" (of, for example, love, divorce, prostitution, the complexes, the accusations and guilt going along with them) is required (cf. *Charmes de Londres (London Charms*, 1,489)). It is true that the casting off of terribly crippling myths and beliefs may involve, for Prévert, direct confrontation, often via quotation, with the perpetrators of these congealing and constraining ideas Prévert is happy to "desert" (cf. 2,255). But Prévert seeks not to *impose* but rather to *depose*, to, above all, testify, and, perhaps, edge from power, those who hold sway over so many minds, blocking the latter's own power, freedom, impulse for joy and innocence. The fundamental "ethical" orientation of Prévert's work, however, allows simply for a full affirmation of the values of freedom, joy, love of life. What better, and wittier, ironic articulation of such values could we hope for than that offered in the opening text of *Histoires et autres histoires*, "Encore une fois sur le fleuve" ("Once More on the River", 1,799), where Poverty's case is pleaded and "its provisional release for an unlimited time" is requested, so that "Justice may be Celebrated". Irony, yes, but, at base, celebration of life is what is at the heart of Prévert's sense of value, celebration and love beyond, and despite, the contradictions within us and without.

> Sur la plus épaisse des soupes théologiques, métaphysiques, scientifiques et reconnues de destruction publique, il y a toujours un cheveu de Vénus.
> (On the thickest of theological, metaphysical, scientific and publicly destructive soups, there is always a hair of Venus.
> Jacques Prévert, *Fatras* (2,49)

AN AESTHETICS OF EMOTION?

We have seen already Prévert's at once smiling and biting satire addressed to the heady intellectualizations and rationalized reductions of life's teeming wonders. It is thus not overly surprising to find him privileging the heart over the mind, or, better, restoring a wise balance between the two, a balance so commonly destroyed by our modern insistence upon the virtues of sheer mental structure, order, orchestration. Emotion, it can often be claimed, can only clutter and hinder, even irritate, like the children who Prévert loves to hear ask awkward questions or "dissociat[e] ideas" (cf. 2,860, *Hebdromadaires*), thus disturbing ideology or the intellectual "alibis" clung to by the intelligentsia (cf. 2,857). Prévert's classic portrayal, in *Spectacle* ("Cas de conscience" ("Guilty Feeling", 1,264-6)), of a woman's emotional life being picked over by "a choir of psychologists comment[ing] on her case", exposes humorously the vulnerabilities of "funereal reason", as he calls it later in the same volume (1,377, "Intermède" ("Interlude")).

This said, however, Prévert remains the least sentimental of poets in the midst of a poetics deconstructing the often pretentious concoctions of the mind and developing in their place a passion and discreet compassion of yet great intensity. Two very early poems from *Paroles* reveal such tautly equilibrated qualities. "La Belle Saison" ("The High Season", 1,16) offers almost exemplary discretion whilst expressing implicitly both compassion and social criticism:

À jeun perdue glacée

Toute seule sans un sou
Une fille de seize ans
Immobile debout
Place de la Concorde
À midi le Quinze Août.
(Hungry lost frozen
All alone without a cent
A sixteen-year-old girl
Standing motionless
On the Place de la Concorde
At noon August fifteenth.)

"Alicante" (1,16) switches the scene to Spain:

Une orange sur la table
Ta robe sur le tapis
Et toi dans mon lit
Doux présent du présent
Fraîcheur de la nuit
Chaleur de ma vie.
(An orange on the table
Your dress on the carpet
And you in my bed
Sweet present of the present
Coolness of the night
Warmth of my life.)

Compassion becomes passion, summer iciness becomes sensual and emotive delight in a summer evening's coolness that is an inner warmth, absence turns to joinedness, the harshness of near-mendicity, even desperate prostitution, to the gentleness of gift. Throughout, however, neither overstatement nor sentimentality. Emotion reigns, the heart is central to Prévert's preoccupations, but there is no narcissism, no self-centeredness: Prévert is not a poet of self-absorbed emotion, but of the emotional life of us all, the universal emotions we share. The *I* multiplies its pertinence and flees above all subjective flagrancy.

The 1960 poem "Cri du coeur" ("Cry from the Heart", 1,897-8), written for Edith Piaf, seems quite explicitly to articulate Prévert's instinctive approach to expression of human emotion. Here is the penultimate stanza:

Sans pitié j'écrase mes larmes
je leur fais pas d'publicité
Si on tirait l'signal d'alarme
pour des chagrins particuliers
jamais les trains ne pourraient rouler
Et je regarde le paysage
si par hasard il est trop laid
j'attends qu'il se r'fasse une beauté
(Pitiless I press back my tears
I don't advertize 'em
If we pulled the emergency cord
for private distress
never could trains keep moving for'd
And I look out at the view
if by chance it's pretty awful
I wait for it to pretty up)

Humor helps, as usual, to put across a vigorous attitude and tackle tricky issues without pointless emotional flabbiness. Upset and grief are not repressed, however, let us note: tears do well up, but, above all, *other* emotions are quickly sought out, so that states are not seen as fixed, but rather ephemeral, changeable, available to our intervention, our action, as well as to our patience - and therefore, implicitly, our confidence. There is nothing facile here, moreover. A poem such as "On" ("Someone", 1,346-7) from *Spectacle* is again wonderfully discreet and intense in its portrayal of a domestic servant's grief in the midst of her humiliation, and, furthermore, she too prefers to swallow her tears and hope - her case is depicted as more desperate - for some "rebirth" of what today is often called, precisely as Prévert pictures it in this poem, her "inner child". No, this is not repression of emotion, but a courageous assumption of all the residual emotional energy within allowing for transcendence and the reaffirmation of the child's magical vision of self and world.

The heart-child figure appears regularly in Prévert's works and can be associated, as in "Chanson de l'oiseleur" ("Song of the Bird-Catcher", 1,105) from *Paroles*, with the exquisite delicacy and strangely fragile strength of a bird. The heart - as the poem tells us - is the place of desire, deep (extralinguistic) self-expression, song, beautiful flight; and this, despite sadness, fear, panic that, bizarrely, are a *part* of its gentleness, its natural rhythmic pulsation. If emotion runs up and down its scales, Prévert, as we shall soon see, is quite clear as to where the best melodies can be played: joy, love, laughter, marvel. But it remains important to stress at this stage of our discussion 1. that Prévert seems fully aware of the role, the purpose of emotions such as melancholy or fear or dislike: they show us what we *don't* want and implicitly remind us of what we *do* want in life; 2. that feeling provides a certainty in regard to being, a certainty curiously unavailable in intellectual terms: the short "Chanson" ("Song", 1,120) from *Paroles* is typically to the point: "We live and we love", Prévert writes, "And we don't know what life is / ... And we don't know what love is"; 3. that emotion, for Prévert, similarly, transcends the relativities of time and language: it is free - again a short poem from *Paroles*, "Le Jardin" ("The Garden", 1,128), beautifully encapsulates the intuition - it is free of the mental categories we create to box it in, free and floating through the mystery of the universe, like the poem's exchanged kiss upon the star we call Earth. No wonder exclamation so often accompanies the expression of emotion: it is the sign both of the latter's intensity and the inadequacy of language to fully speak it. No wonder, either, that in the poem "Boris Vian", dedicated to his friend and immediate neighbor, Prévert argues that "people said of him that he was headstrong / [but that] regardless of what they said / his heart above all determined what he did" (*Fatras*, 2,118). Vian: a writer of feeling and heart, ironically dead before reaching the age of forty of cardiac problems, leaving behind him, as will Prévert some eighteen years on, a lucid but heartfelt and heart-warming oeuvre. "He loved [life]/ as he loved love / like a real deserter of unhappiness"(2,119).

COMPLICATION, (COM)PASSION

Robert Desnos, an early friend from Prévert's Surrealist years, is described in *Hebdromadaires* (2,917) as a "man of merry unhappiness", a description which serves to remind us of Prévert's consciousness of the complex, heterogeneous and involute nature of emotion. If there are profound things in Miró's aesthetics which Prévert may deem "elementary", he knows too that radiance and bloodiness can mingle in the realm of dream and imaginative errancy (cf. 2,524). Emotional range, in effect, would seem to imply, for Prévert, various factors - perhaps simply questions? -: of fluctuation;

of simultaneity or com-*pli*-cation, one emotion *folded* into another; of transformation; of choice or submission, default. To move from one poem to the next may produce an overall map of the sentiments human beings may experience, from dismay and anger, melancholy and anxiety, to relief or cynicism, ease and exuberance. But Prévert's work as a whole, and the individual texts, short and long, that make it up, also portray ceaselessly, not just the variance, the dipping and soaring of human affectivity, but the real or possible simultaneity, within the *same* individual, of conflicting, yet also strangely complementary emotions. The poem written for Edith Piaf to sing, "Cri du coeur"(1,897-8), shows amply such simultaneity - of upset and grief, will and possibility - and demonstrates too that where there is simultaneity, there is option, choice, conceivable self-transformation, conceivable self-abandonment - all, in Prévert, moreover, beyond moralization and judgement. "Le Désespoir est assis sur un banc" ("Despair is Sitting on a Bench", 1,104), from *Paroles* is the poem of the *felt* impossibility of transforming the mask of smile into a true, lived smile that can ease suffering and give back to the man portrayed those child- and bird-like qualities he risks losing forever. The much celebrated poem from the same volume, "Le Cancre" ("The Dunce", 1,43), becomes, on the other hand, the poem of (self-)affirmation in the midst of much that could readily have undermined it. It shows that laughter and joy - crucial factors of Prévert's ontology (- and how he would laugh at that word!) - constitute a vaster and deeper intelligence than anything represented by the teacher and the bright students who mock:

> Il dit non avec la tête
> mais il dit oui avec le coeur
> il dit oui à ce qu'il aime
> il dit non au professeur
> il est debout
> on le questionne
> et tous les problèmes sont posés
> soudain le fou rire le prend
> et il efface tout
> les chiffres et les mots
> les dates et les noms
> les phrases et les pièges
> et malgré les menaces du maître
> sous les huées des enfants prodiges

avec des craies de toutes les couleurs
sur le tableau noir du malheur
il dessine le visage du bonheur
(He shakes his head
but nods with his heart
he says yes to what he likes
he says no to the teacher
he stands there
being questioned
and all problems are put to him
suddenly he can't stop laughing
and he erases everything
numbers and words
dates and names
sentences and traps
and in spite of the master's threats
amidst the jeers of the child prodigies
with chalk of every color
on the blackboard of calamity
he draws the face of happiness.)

If Prévert left school at fourteen he did so with his *certificat d'études* as many bright young adolescents did then and do even now, all over the world. If he found school limiting, he certainly didn't find it difficult or particularly unpleasant, on a strictly personal level (cf. *Hebdromadaires* (passim)). But of course, the above poem is not what Michel Deguy calls a "self-story", it is a poem of observation, at once bearing witness and symbolic: bearing witness to the possible cruelties and futilities of education, its inflexibilities, its waste, its often complete lack of understanding of what truly matters and what can be accomplished with young people and their bubbling energies greatly in excess of the narrow focus of substance and treatment generally afforded them. The so-called dunce - who is simply a human being not well suited to what may suit other people (who, in turn, may be unsuited to what suits him or her) - "says no" to (rejects / cannot cope with / is ill-suited to) particular forms of analysis, memory and no doubt psychology, manner, which could lead to his or her unhappiness. What, fortunately and symbolically, *le cancre* achieves is a display of "heart", of good will, an affirmation of what (s)he "likes, of what corresponds to the strengths, the energies, the loves within, which, in turn, constitute a portrayal of his or her capacity for happiness.

Prévert, in "Le Cancre", reveals at once his compassion for all those children and adolescents who would like nothing better than to excel but who would like to show that there are many *different* hoops to jump through. The poem is an *ideal* emblem, of course, in that it recognizes and depicts what many children in such situations may not be quite capable of depicting in an educational setting: their passion for life, their personal power, their wonderful emotional intelligence in concentrating upon love and joy.

Compassion, com-passion: a sympathetic sharing of the understood, the so easily repressed, even denigrated passion for life of the other. In *Grand Bal du Printemps*, Prévert quotes Melville (in French, my translation) as saying that "passion, and passion at its deepest, is not a thing demanding a palatial stage upon which to act itself out. In the underworld, amongst beggars and those sifting through garbage, deep passion reigns"(1,447). Prévert's sometimes touted "indifference" - *learned*, he argues, and learned young to protect against an empathy and a sensitivity that, taken to extremes, could clearly have traumatized him - is the ironic, now cynical, now simply smiling, *other side* of his vast and undying, laughing passion for life and recognition of the latter in others including those, like the "dunce", like those spotted by Melville, whose great vital energy may either be so enfolded in, so complicated by, problem or so disregarded by their intellectual "superiors" that their natural emotional poetry can wither and die. This Georges Bataille appreciates too, amazed as he is at the extraordinary dovetailing of intense passion and complete lack of seriousness Prévert can bring about in a flash.

FEAR, (SELF-)PUNISHMENT

Frequently, Prévert's writings draw attention to the anxious, fearful state of mind that dominates in modern society. His wonderful 1971 collaboration with Alexander Calder, *Fêtes (Celebrations)* argues, for example, that "there is always in the warmest wish [of *Homo Sapiens* - what a strange label!] a fleeting anxiety" (2,205). Doubt and fear so commonly sap the emotional ground on which he, or she, stands. For Prévert, moreover, such fear represents to some considerable degree a refusal of the light and heat within the self. The 1936 poems Prévert wrote in Ibiza and handed to Guy Lévis Mano only to forget them until long after the war - 1955, in fact - touch firmly on this ticklish issue. We read for example in the middle of the rather long opening, eponymous text of *Lumières d'homme* (1,630-31) this passage which I should like to quote extensively for its both particular and global pertinence:

je hurle à la lumière avec de l'encre et du papier
le soir tard
et je crie
tout de même
il y a la lumière
chacun a sa lumière
et le monde crève de froid
le monde a peur de se brûler les doigts
évidemment
c'est la lumière qui brille qui brûle qui fait cuire
et qui glace le sang
c'est la grande omelette surprise
le soileil avec des caillots de sang
lueur du coeur
lueur de l'amour
lueur
oh il faut la poursuivre cette lueur aveuglante
elle existe
elle crève les yeux
mais s'il faut que les yeux crèvent pour tout voir
crevez les yeux

c'est la lumière vivante que chacun porte en soi
et que tout le monde étouffe pour faire comme tout le
  monde.
(I yell out to the light with ink and paper
late at night
and I cry out
all the same
there's the light
everyone has his or her light
and the world is dying from cold
the world is afraid of burning its fingers
obviously
it's the light that shines burns cooks

and chills the blood
it's the big surprise omelette
the sun with blood clots
glimmer of the heart
glimmer of love
glimmering
you must, yes, pursue this blinding glimmer of light
it exists
it's staring you in the face
but if you must put out your eyes to see everything
put them out

it's the living light each of us bears within
and everyone smothers so as not to be different)

This, in substantial part then, is the poem of our frequently manifest fear of our own full potential, our full and passionate embrace of our being, our full self-affirming illumination that can blind us yet bring us revelation, self-revelation, full access to the dazzling, surprising realms of the "heart" and of love. All too often, the self accepts limits in this fear of its own limitlessness, limits that somehow, whether ideological, political, psychological, even physical, provide a compacted space of being, perhaps reassuring yet also frustrating, congealing, unavailable to the suppleness of being within and around the self in others. Fear, as Prévert says in "Sait-on jamais?" ("You Never Know", 2,225) from *Choses et autres*, can push us to articulating certainties where, in effect, and happily, none exist: "They say they always know / They say the earth the moon the cosmos infinity good evil and the origins of life / They say everything as if there was nothing to it" - but, as Prévert continues, freedom, openness, unfathomable mystery strangely terrifies: "but when apprehensiveness over incomprehension grabs them / they're afraid / and this fear overturns the vaporousness of their ideas".

Such fear, of course, then is implicitly directed towards the very belief systems, our "ideas" that, no longer, can contain and constrain the world experienced. Whilst this *may* lead to a questioning of one's self-imposed conceptual limits - and Prévert proposes a crash course in "civic education" in *Fatras* (2,13): "After fear of death, death of fear, and finally life"- more often than not Prévert observes in human behavior a relinquishing of the freedom feasible via such questioning, and the firming-up of an alternately self-punishing/punishing psychology. Various poems are devoted to this phenomenon or evoke it en passant. "Mauvaise soirée" ("Rough Night", 1,636-40), for example, in *Lumières d'homme* proclaims that "men don't seem / to want to stop suffering / and I'm one of those men / men don't seem / to want to stop causing suffering / what's got into them / all those people..." (1,639). Such masochism - and, indeed, sadism - has, quite simply, the poem finally confirms, been learned, and, if teaching and indoctrination play a role, learning also involves clearly choice and personal responsibility in Prévert's eyes. To cease to fear - and, as we have just seen, Prévert does not place himself on some pedestal of ideal self-actualization: he, too, experiences the challenge of surmounting fear - involves letting go of the impulse to criticize, accuse and punish both the self and others. It demands the (self-)love and care (again, for self *and* others) that is seen as an essential remedy in the short text "Pourquoi souffrir..." ("Why Suffer...", 2,813), published in 1955, with lithographs by Chagall, Braque and Segonzac, to support the cause of socially maladjusted children. "Loving [them], caring for [them], restoring [them] / there is no other answer" Prévert concludes. Fear, in these equations, always involves a lack of self-esteem or esteem for the other, or both. Its dissolution comes via respect, love, (com)passion, a will for joy. And via the embrace of what I shall now term "marvel".

THE MARVELOUS

The Surrealists, of course, speak much of *le merveilleux* and indeed it is an element found all the way back in ancient myths as well as in more modern mutations in the literature of, say, the allegorically symbolist, the fantastic or even science-fiction. To some extent regardless of the specific literary time-frame or modal application, the marvelous tends to deploy itself in the realms of the magical and the fabulous, the astonishingly inexplicable and what Aragon, in *Le Paysan de Paris (Paris Peasant)*, called "contradiction appearing in reality". Prévert's own sense of the marvelous fits with much of this, but is, typically, more absolutely rooted in the intrinsic strangeness of the "ordinary", whilst displaying at times a nice parodic twist. Take "J'en ai vu plusieurs..." ("I saw several...", 1,27), from the opening pages of *Paroles*, where the *je* of the poem narrates his or her observations of the banal, at times conceivably tragic, but also (implicitly) bizarrely fatuous, or perhaps even (simply) magically human gestures and acts - seen almost as if by a puzzled alien. The poem ends:

> J'en ai vu un qui tirait son enfant par la main
> et qui criait...
> j'en ai vu un avec un chien
> j'en ai vu un avec une canne à épée
> j'en ai vu un qui pleurait
> j'en ai vu un qui entrait dans une église
> j'en ai vu un autre qui en sortait...
> (I saw one pulling along his child by the hand
> and shouting...
> I saw one with a dog
> I saw one with a sword-stick
> I saw one crying
> I saw one going into a church
> I saw another one coming out...)

It is, moreover, clear from this example that what Prévert may deem to partake of the marvelous, may be positively *or* negatively connoted. In this sense the strangeness of life, whether ethically, emotionally desirable or not, may retain a certain marvelousness and provoke sentiments of astonishment - either openly or implicitly parodic, or accompanied by admiration and an overt enthusiasm lacking in "J'en ai vu plusieurs...". The strange, the enigmatic - and, for Prévert, what, at bottom, is not strange and enigmatic in life? - *are what is*: the "demons and marvels / Winds and tides" of a person's half-open eyes, for example, the "quicksands" of being's material signs in which the mind can so easily "drown" (cf. "Sables mouvants" ("Quicksands", 1,107), *Paroles*).

It is true that, in *Choses et autres*, Prévert can affirm that "there are not five or six wonders of the world, but only one: love" (2,273). But this is, as it were, shorthand, a compacting into a symbolic absolute of all that Prévert deems remarkable, fascinating, "loveable" in life, worthy of celebration - even via his endless ironic "counter-celebrations" which, invertedly, sing the praises, in effect, of love and joy. *Grand Bal du printemps* (1,437), for example, opens thusly:

Sur une palissade
dans un pauvre quartier
des affiches mal collées
Grand Bal du Printemps
illuminent
l'ombre d'un arbre décharné
et celle d'un réverbère pas encore allumé

Devant ces petites annonces de la vie
un passant s'est arrêté
émerveillé
(On a fence
in a poor district
posters coming unstuck
Great Spring Ball
light up
the shadow of a scraggy tree
and that of a street lamp not yet lit

Before these small ads of life
a passer-by has stopped
full of wonder)

The marvelous blossoming away in the midst of deprivation, showing its promise, its power of spring-like renascence, its capacity to illuminate even the drabbest existence... Moreover, it is not just a question of contrast: a festive dance to alleviate the wretchedness of the underprivileged; in Prévert, such signs remain emblematic of feasible inner developments and transformations of a more ongoing nature: life as permanent marvel, as an astonishing, exhilarating dance of being - often against the odds. Izis' photographs, freely associated with Prévert's poems in *Grand Bal du Printemps*, clearly portray the magicalness of presence, human and non-human, over and above the socio-economic constraints they may indirectly also represent. The wondrous, the prodigious, reside, as another early poem, from *Paroles* readily shows, not in an insistence on the contradictions of moralizing neighbors watching a young adolescent girl traverse their dirt-poor street, but in the inwardly felt joy and pride experienced at the sight "of your dazzling beauty / your provocative youthfulness / your marvelous poverty / your marvelous freedom" ("La Rue de Buci maintenant..." ("Rue de Buci Now...",

1,136)). A strange and fabulous maximum at the heart of some apparent minimum; a maximum that adults may be so often tempted to deny, accuse, denigrate, trapped as they may be in their many ideologies, but which they know to exist as a true marvel...

Children, as ever, great artists too, and poets, perhaps pushing aside the masks of conventional belief and interpretation, looking lucidly and lovingly at the world, marvelling at its swirling strangeness like Miró "ever smiling faithfully and gravely / ever in awe" ("Romancero Miró", 2,523) - such people run little risk of forgetting the truth and the beauty of the real, of the everyday. They see what "few can see"; they know - but beyond proof - "what few can know", as Prévert writes of the child whose nose is pressed against the window of life's astonishments (*Grand Bal du Printemps*, 2,463); they imagine freely invisible wonders of mind and heart, and sing them unhesitatingly in joy together (cf. *ibid*,464):

Au coin d'la rue du Jour
et d'la rue Paradis
j'ai vu passer un homme
y a que moi qui l'ai vu
j'ai vu passer un homme
tout nu en plein midi
y a que moi qui l'ai vu
pourtant c'est moi l'plus petit
les grands y savent pas voir
surtout quand c'est marrant surtout quand c'est joli

Il avait des ch'veux d'ange
une barbe de fleuve
une grande queue de sirène
une taille de guêpe
....
(At the corner of Day Street
an' Paradise Street
I saw a man go by
only I saw 'im
I saw a man go by
stark naked in broad daylight
only I saw 'im
yet I'm the littlest
grown-ups can't see
specially when it's funny specially when it's nice

51

He had angel 'air
a flowing beard
a great mermaid's tail
a waspy waist
.....................)

And so on: Louis XIII chair legs, a body like a poplar trunk, a "finger of wine", and, from there, the metaphors and wordplay cascade in increasing merriment and delight in the marvelous.

No, Prévert is not, as he wittily points out to André Pozner in *Hebdromadaires*, a poet of righteous, moral or amoral indignation: "as dignity makes me laugh, indignation has always been foreign to me" (2,833); his deep and constant desire is to draw our attention to the innocent, puzzling, yet wondrously exhilarating amazements of "ordinary" life. The difficulties and challenges of the latter are never underestimated by Prévert, but neither would he ever have us forget the marvelousness in the bosom of existence, that marvelousness so finely evoked throughout the opening poem of *Histoires et autres histoires*, "Encore une fois sur le fleuve", and especially in its conclusion, with its scene of love made on a cement bag:

> N'oublie pas l'astre de ceux qui s'aiment
> l'astre de l'instant même et de l'éternité
> l'étourdissante étoile du plaisir partagé
>
> Qui pourrait jamais l'oublier
> (Don't forget the star of those in love
> the star of the very moment and eternity
> the giddying star of shared pleasure
>
> Who could ever forget it)

Who? Why, any of us, clinging to an idea, neglecting what truly matters to us, losing contact with love, "the only [wonder of the world]"...

LAUGHTER

The laughter of Braque and Picasso, together in Saint-Paul-de-Vence, says Prévert, who knew them well enough, is not derisive, dismissive, scornful: it is, rather, of the kind that appeals to Prévert, frank, exuberant, a release, a free self-expression and a joy, like their act of painting itself (cf. "De vive joie" ("By Word of Joy", 2,570)). Laughter, too, for the Surrealists, Prévert sees, and experienced personally, as an all-penetrating phenomenon, "agressively salubrious and undeniably contagious" (2,915) - like the laughter of his friend and co-poet André Verdet, neither threatening nor triumphant (cf. "C'est à Saint-Paul-de-Vence"("It's in Saint-Paul-de-Vence", 1,883)). All in all, it constitutes a fundamental element of Prévert's personal arsenal and an element that, as in "La Rue de Buci maintenant...", may determine via its presence or absence, the veritable character of a place and its micro-society: "poor odd and malnourished street / your bread has been taken from your mouth / your ovaries have been torn out / the grass has been cut from under your feet / your songs have been pushed back down your throat / your gaiety has been removed / and the diamond of your laughter has broken its teeth on the iron curtain of bloody nonsense and hatred" (1,134, *Paroles*). Laughter, then, as, hopefully, but by no means assuredly, as this poem shows us, a guarantee against *la connerie et la haine*.

Whilst Prévert's own modes of laughter are extremely varied and of course find their roots in the work of many writers of both French and other traditions - from the raucous yet pointed buffoonery of a Rabelais, the balletic satire of a Molière, the light badinage of a Marivaux, through the magical dream-scenes of which Shakespeare was capable or the smilingly fertile fusings of the real and the imagined of the admired Cervantes, to the tight ironies of a Baudelaire, the contemporary tensions and great guffawing release available in writers as different as Jarry, Vian or Beckett - whilst these and other loose affinities inevitably may be reasonably and pertinently argued, it is not my purpose here to plunge into endless comparisons and contrasts, or even definitory endeavors. Rather what interests me, and what I can only very briefly sketch out, is the emotional and psychic pertinence of laughter for Prévert. And of a particularly visceral, explosive laughter, that of *le fou rire*, rhythmic, near-uncontrollable, no longer constrained by circumstance or creed, given over to the intrinsic joy it carries, whether purely silly or socially conscious at some level.

Le fou rire abounds in both Prévert's poems and his memoirs. The "dunce" of *Paroles*, we recall, bursts the shackles of socio-psychological oppression and exclusion by, precisely, *erasing* their symbols and "drawing the face of happiness" in their place (1,43). *Le fou rire* is an emblem and an actual avenue of self-transformation for all those *fous de misère*, all those people wild with wretchedness, powerfully depicted in *Grand Bal du Printemps* in the poem of that title (1,456-8). At best such people cling "to life / [via] a childish hope [keeping] them company", but they cannot assume quite the full "childishness", that vast and absolute freedom, of young children and adolescents laughing gaily - on a Sunday, moreover - as they dance along the no doubt symbolic as well as real *rue de la Paix* wearing their "coats of uncontrollable laughter", "wild children from the upper city"(1,479).

Prévert remembers with affection, towards the end of his life, his mother's laughter:

> Quand dans la rue, au marché, ou n'importe où, on lui disait qu'elle était belle, un peu gênée, elle rosissait puis éclatait de rire: « C'est le fou rire », disait-elle, « je l'avais déjà toute petite et toujours à n'en plus finir. C'est plus fort que moi, plus fort que les larmes que j'ai jamais versées ». Et le fou rire me prenant à mon tour, elle ajoutait: « Tu vois, c'est contagieux. Il y en a qui attrapent froid et d'autres la gaieté... ».
>
> (When in the street, at the market, or anywhere, people told her she was beautiful, a little embarrassed she would turn pink then burst out laughing: "I can't stop", she would say, "I was already like that when I was little and it was always never-ending. I can't control it, it's more uncontrollable than all the tears I've ever shed". And, bursting into a fit of laughter myself, she would add: "It's contagious, you know. There are some who catch cold and others high spirits...")

Such laughter may be sparked off by an amusing turn of phrase or the incongruousness of converging factors, but, *ideally*, as here, it is the sign of a shared intrinsic, instinctual will for joy, for love, a bursting recognition of the available beauties of life. *Ideally*, as the wonderful, thoroughly delightful "Anabiose" ("Anabiosis", 2,94-100) from *Fatras* suggests, laughter and *le fou rire* especially constitute a "return to life", a tonic revival of the jubilating energies within, a mass popular movement or revolutionary uprising that, truly, is "angelic" - a true social progress. And therefore, as "Anabiose" points out in this witty scenario, a movement which those in power, in control (of themselves and others), seek to stamp out. This is not the soured, sad, ironic laughter of the woman of "Où je vais, d'où je viens" ("Where I'm Going, Where I Come From") from *La Pluie et le beau temps*, who can only "laugh at everything and everything and everything", because she has lost everything and, above all, "the only man I loved / ... / beaten to a pulp, trodden down... / finished off" (1,718). The splendidly envisioned laughter of the people of "Anabiose", or of Prévert's adored mother, is the laughter linking up with the very forces of the cosmos, as Prévert sees them, forces at once wild and wise, free to laugh with their inherently exuberant bent for radiance. "A wild wind coming from the sea", he writes in the fine collaboration with Ribemont-Dessaignes, *Arbres*, "howls sings out and whistles and laughs away" (2,147)... A laughter of freshness, making and unmaking life's boundless music... For Prévert, such laughter is the best way to go, as an aphoristic *inédit* affirms (2,945):

> Mourra bien qui rira le dernier
> ([S]he who dies best laughs last.)

(SELF-)LOVE

Love, Prévert argues, has over the years not had a good press and has often generated suspicion, derision, coldness, hatred - despite the appropriations inflicted on it: "this word they have for the most part denatured dissected sacralized denied capitalized megalomanized", he writes in *Fatras* ("A...", 2,125). For Prévert, however, love is at once indispensable and inexplicable, simple, whether manifest, as he says with a characteristic wink and smile, "in bed [or] on earth" ("Les Chiens ont soif" ("The Dogs are Thirsty", 2,87). It thus remains for him outside of the scope of morality and royally free of all ideological exploitation men and women yet so commonly continue to impose on it. Quoting Blake in an epigraph to one of the many pieces composing *Charmes de Londres* (*London Charms*) – "Better to suffocate a child in the crib than cradle unsatisfied desires" (my translation) – Prévert whimsically and yet meaningfully concludes:

N'écoutez pas Monsieur Loyal
n'écoutez pas Monsieur Légal
n'attendez pas qu'il règle votre entrée sur la piste
Aimez-vous dès maintenant
et ne faites pas semblant aimez-vous tout de suite
(Don't listen to Mister Loyal
don't listen to Mister Legal
don't wait for him to regulate your entrance onto the track
Love each other right away
and don't pretend love each other straight away)

Beyond moral niceties, urgent, animal yet psychically central and centering, love for Prévert is both a raw and subtle dance of being (cf. "Sanguine" ("Blood Orange") or "Il a tourné autour de moi" ("He Moved About me"), 1,330-31). Unfathomable, because rationally irreducible, yet stunningly real, love - like laughter and joy - works spontaneously against what Prévert calls, in the very witty "C'était en l'an vingt-deux..." ("It is was in the year twenty-two...") from *Spectacle*, that so prevalent, so needlessly unhappy "Morticulture" (1,384). In so doing, it works against temporality, or life seen as a constant declining, and rather "for life", "because of life", as Prévert puts it in *Grand Bal du Printemps* (1,474). Love's time is not counted in minutes, any more than it is bound by frontiers, spatial or other (cf. "A...", 2,129). Love, rather, seems to Prévert to open a vast, infinitely expandable and ever urgent non-space-time, a vital psychic, emotional *now* which he evokes at the end of the poem named after its last line from *Histoires et autres histoires* (1,851):

Notre vie c'est maintenant
Embrasse-moi!
(Our life is now
Kiss me!)

It is not, of course, that love cannot have its high and low states, ebb and flow. But, as it were, within that temporality, love's true presence yet eludes the constraints and the very framework that seem to have generated it. Thus does a poem such as "Cet amour" ("This Love") from *Paroles* unhesitatingly situate love within the framework of ephemerality and change, yet at the same time characterize it as unchanging, true, eternally available, constant, a salvatory phenomenon ever within us even if we may think it lies without (cf. 1,97-99). No *deus/dea ex machina* for Prévert...

We are, in effect, the machine and the god(dess) and both their potential names are love. To love, then, involves not simply waiting for a solution to its seeming absence to arrive from the outside. Love depends, to some critical degree for Prévert, on a love of the self, a love thriving freely within the self, which is not egotistical, narcissistic according to any conventional definition, but which constitutes a recognition of the worth, beauty, power of transcendence *and* simple, exquisite immanence curiously, mysteriously invested within each person. "She comes, she is more beautiful and better developed than ever", the narrator of "Éclaircie" ("Clearing", 1,664) says of the woman he awaits in the subway, "she smiles, she is happy, she understands everything, she knows everything, she loves me as much as I love her and, as I do myself, she also loves herself very much". If this seems an ideal scenario, it is nonetheless one possessing great truth in Prévert's eyes. So-called self-love – as I have described it above – sets love, the love of the other, the recognition of the status of the other's being, free. If jealousy – "the cold stone of jealousy / upon the reflection / of your beauty", as Prévert writes in *La Pluie et le beau temps* – can be experienced, it can thus be understood to involve a loosening recognition of one's own worth, power, etc., a slippage in one's self-love, a diminution of the love naturally generated within the self. Similarly, possession of the other is not part of Prévert's conception of ideal love. "You don't belong to me", he happily concludes in "Belle" ("Beautiful", 2,388) from the 1975 *Le Jour des temps (The Day of Times)*, finely illustrated by Max Papart, "though you're the only desert island on which I could live with you". No, love, in a most curious way, concerns the self first, the other clearly, but in an utterly liberating fashion, and all others uninvolved not at all. "Je suis comme je suis" ("I am the Way I am", 1,66) from *Paroles* firmly articulates this latter point. Love *is*, absolute, childlike, innocent, unrequiring of commentary, regardless of its social context, free, self-determined, self-determining. For Prévert, it involves at root, and unless perverted from the inside or the outside by a lack of esteem/self-esteem, a natural expression of the self's energies, as in "Encore une fois sur le fleuve" (1,803), an expression of being *sufficient unto itself*. It is a phenomenon Prévert observes, moreover, at the heart of, say, Miró's painting (cf. "Romancero Miró", 2,524) - "Miró loves life / life loves Miró / life loves love / it's elementary"- or as being central to the poetic act as André Verdet also conceives it - "he wanders about in his poems in search of what he loves" ("C'est à Saint-Paul-de-Vence", 1,885). And, indeed, ultimately, love must represent a broad and passionate, uncontrolling, free embrace of life, its manifold forms and states, an embrace as joyous as possible, as uncomplicating as possible. If only, Prévert says with irresistible wit and his usual dig in a fragment André Pozner publishes in 1982, "if only they had counted the centuries after Eros or Venus instead of according to Jesus Christ, we wouldn't be where we are now" (2,936). *Love*, a force of mighty deconstruction, the great energy lighting our strange and marvelous ways.

FESTIVITY, JOY

But if love lights our way(s), where might the latter lead? For Prévert, the answer lies, I should argue, both in the self-sufficiency of love's "logic" *and* in its quasi-synonymity with joy and (self-) celebration.

Certainly, Prévert's work as a whole, poetic, filmic, autobiographical, critical, never ceases to privilege a thematics of festivity, *fête*, personal, collective, even cosmic revelry - a merry-making at once ordinary and profound in its significance. "Fiesta", for example, from *Histoires et autres histoires*, gives us the poem of the feast of love, its intimacy, its inimitable intensity (cf. 1,819). "Jour de fête" ("Holiday"), from the same collection - reminiscent via its title of Hugo's wonderful "Jour de fête aux environs de Paris" ("Holiday in the Vicinity of Paris"), a poem surely admired by Prévert the "proletarian"- recounts the improbable but marvelous celebration by a child of a frog's "birthday", a "heartfelt" celebration that parents and family do not appreciate and seek to stifle (cf. 1,825-6). "La Fête à Neuilly" ("Neuilly Fair"), still from the 1946/1963 volume, offers a more characteristic context of festivity, that of a fair, but eludes the obvious in showing us its early morning departure, leaving the waking, perhaps still expectant children without their lions and pelicans and monkeys. Poems such as the long "C'est à Saint-Paul-de-Vence..." (1,874-86) or texts recounting Prévert's childhood and youth in "Enfance" (2,216-17) give us an almost classic and idyllic portrayal of fairs and festive occasions, street vending, acting, showpersonship, open-air dances and so on, and these scenes often merge in Prévert's mind with theatrical performance and life, even his experience - as a child spectator - of the nascent world of cinema. Always, ordinary working people spin and turn and jubilate at the center of such festivity. As Prévert writes in *Grand Bal du Printemps* (1,470), "people are the ones who create fun / conjure it with their hands make it alive with their laughter pay for it in cash parade through it their loves their wives their children // People create fun /others just pretend".

Prévert, despite his often satirical purposing and his at times acerbic irony, is a man ever on the lookout for the buoyant, exhilarating experience of having fun, creating fun *(faire la fête)*. The trees depicted by Ribemont-Dessaignes and beautifully evoked by Prévert in *Arbres* (2,158) are, somehow, always

> Des arbres en goguette en fête
> en liberté
> (Trees in merriment festive mood
> freedom).

When he regards, similarly, Alexander Calder's paintings or sculptures, he again sees them as a vast and teeming celebration of color, form and life's energies. The swirling or even stationary presence, both of nature and antinature or art, strikes Prévert as a wondrous fount of being, quite independent, and joyously so, of the pure intellectual, aesthetic or even utilitarian equations we might be tempted to place upon it. Trees, paintings – just like wild animals or children or women, all the endless phenomena of a world we only think we understand – seen by Prévert as a vast circus or fair of being, marvelous, there for the taking, the enjoyment, yet endlessly free, part of "the fair of daily life", as he says in *Charmes de Londres*, part of that idyllic potential lying at the heart of existence which can be, as *Lettre des îles Baladar* tells us, "festivity at the slightest occasion" (1,531)...

The greatest emotion achievable, for Prévert, undoubtedly is this festive joy, this jubilation in the mystery of being. "Fête foraine" ("Fun Fair") from *Paroles* conveys this unambiguously. The poem begins:

> Heureux comme la truite remontant le torrent

Heureux le coeur du monde
Sur son jet d'eau de sang
Heureux le limonaire
Hurlant dans la poussière
De sa voix de citron
Un refrain populaire
Sans rime ni raison
Heureux les amoureux
Sur les montagnes russes
(Happy as a trout swimming back upstream
Happy the world's heart
Upon its spurting fountain of blood
Happy the barrel-organ
grinding out in the dust
Of its baritone voice
A popular refrain
Without rhyme or reason
Happy the lovers
In the Russian mountains),

and finally gathers into its fold of festive planetary happiness and recuperative laughter, young and old, fat and thin, babies and idiots (cf. 1,123). For, at its center, its core, Prévert insists, here as elsewhere, the world *is* happy, joyous. Joy *is* available, if, like the street cleaner sweeping the gutter and suddenly seeing a statue, or Prévert the street cleaner looking in amazement at Paul Klee's paintings, we open ourselves to it, are prepared to intuit it, become "inexplicably happy" (cf. "Parfois le balayeur" ("Sometimes the Sweeper"), 1,361-2).

As we saw in *Grand Bal du Printemps*, however, such joy is not, cannot be, a pretence. It is spontaneous, "spurting", vital, far from the *petit bonheur* Anouilh evokes in *Antigone*, and available both to our will and our trust. The poem of Tom, the Harlem shoe-shine man, from *Histoires et autres histoires*, emphasises these latter factors as Tom "sings of the joy of living / The joy of making love and the joy of dancing / And then the joy of being drunk / And the joy of singing" (1,830). And André Pozner tells us of the reaction of Prévert himself, "exclaim[ing] with real joy when a friend would call him, even in the midst of worries, work, especially in the midst of work" (2,867). Joy, happiness, merriment, laughter, fused with love, are for Prévert the very stuff of life: he opposes them gaily to the destructive creations of "great scientific minds exercis[ing] their wits perfecting new bacteriological weapons" ("Bacilles" ("Germs"), 2,179); he very rightly stresses in the same collection, *Imaginaires*, the degree to which "in most great writings expressing or oppressing ideas, the word happiness is denied, mocked, whereas the word unhappiness [*malheur*] almost always holds a place of honor"(2,166); he commonly generates witty and pointed aphorisms to insist upon the beauty, the liberty, the unpretentiousness of natural happiness: "The games of Faith [*Foi*] are mere ashes in comparison with the flames of Joy [*Joie*]", he writes for example in *Spectacle* (1,381). Yes, provocatively, some might feel, the great emotion of joy is, in Prévert's eyes, a matter of confidence and will, self-protection, self-creation. He quotes in "Carmina Burana" from *Choses et autres* (2,270) an "old Chinese proverb":

« Si tu veux être heureux sois-le! »
("If you want to be happy be happy!")

As with a poet such as Yves Bonnefoy, ontological affirmation and consent are crucial and they are intentions, thoughts, best propelled by the energy of emotion, of the heart. "Yes to things and beings", Prévert suggests in the tellingly titled "Maintenant j'ai grandi" ("Now I've grown up", 1,673-4), "to beings and things to be looked at caressed / loved / there for the taking or the leaving". Like Bonnefoy, too – and both poets may be said to echo after their fashion the Rimbaud of "Dévotion"– Prévert concludes by stressing the extent to which such *assent to presence* coincides with a refusal of concept, "ideal ideas", any ideas that could imprison, devour his freedom, his openness to the mystery of being. Such a refusal, he knows, is not easily maintained, but Prévert remains vigilant in the face of any ideational, intellectual, ideological fixities, fixations: if they lie in wait for him, so does he for them (cf. 1,674). His joy, his affirmation of joy, exuberance, love, freedom, are feasible only at the price of such vigilance – which is synonymous with the very confidence in the *joie de vivre* he intuits, wills and creates.

EARTH

il garde grande ouverte sa
fenêtre qui donne sur la mer,
sur la terre, sur la vie
(he keeps wide open his
window overlooking the sea,
the earth, life.)
Jacques Prévert,
Fatras (2,53)

PROFUNDITY, BEAUTY

The work of Prévert – poem, play, screenplay, prose, collage, "graffiti" and so on – is not centered upon the formal nicety, the intellectual prestige, the esoteric challenge of its production. His is not a work seeking some aesthetic, purely textual pleasure narcissistically admiring its own various and self-sufficient accomplishments and contentedly, proudly even, cutting itself off from a world, an earth, to which its deems itself superior. If it concerns itself with questions of beauty and profundity, it thus tends to see these qualities as belonging, really or potentially, to the earth at large and by no means as located within the strict confines of work, image, text, book. The latter orient themselves not inwardly, in a shimmer of self-reflexivity; they are, rather, extroverted, transitive, not really interested in their own aesthetic closure, but eager instead to reengage us in a simple, enthused and bright-eyed, ever marvelling reading of what, in *Arbres*, Prévert calls the "great treatise" (2,152), ancient and deep-rooted, of the earth. If a poem or a painting can be beautiful - and Prévert's many writings on the artists he knew and admired demonstrate how this clearly can be so –, they are principally beautiful for Prévert not because they establish a detached interior exquisiteness, but because they open our minds and hearts to the intrinsic beauty of nature's colors, shapes, textures, the joy and exuberance available in that "first great serial or soap opera"(2,153) that, for him, is the world, its natural phenomena, creatures, beings. "Beauty", Prévert writes in his marvellously self-illustrated "Premier test des amants" ("First Test for Lovers", 2,116) from *Fatras* –

"Beauty [is] not imaginary, that's why nowadays it still roams the earth".

"Vignette pour les vignerons"("Vignette for Wine Growers", 1,680-84), from *La Pluie et le beau temps* is a typical example of this conception of where true beauty and profundity can be best located, sought, felt and fostered. The poem, headed by an epigraph from Hugo whom Prévert clearly admires for his celebration of the everyday gestures, acts and, above all, pleasures of ordinary people, *is* a vignette, a kind of "text illustration", a decorative flourish become literary sketch. As such it could choose to invite us above all to appreciate its artifice, its *own* charm and subtle delights, perhaps over-developing them at the expense of the fragment of the world the vignette yet draws upon. Prévert's poem, however, offers no such ambiguity; its purpose is to sing and "illustrate", "sketch out", the real, natural and profound simplicities, and beauties, of people, wine growers, close to the earth, celebrating its bounty, its mystery, its immense joyousness. The vignette is *for* the wine growers: art, not for art's sake, but for the real, the earth, the gritty, earthy experience of life.

If Prévert is, in effect, a "popular" poet – the most popular by far of his century and second only to Victor Hugo – it is no doubt in part because of the above factors. He is a poet speaking to people of any walk of life, so often about their myriad situations in everyday life, speaking with the vigor, wit and spontaneous dynamism of ordinary, "popular" speech, speaking unpretentiously, both sympathetically and provocatively, unsentimentally, pushily and enthusiastically about life as, at bottom, we know and recognise it. The beauties and profundities of daily existence, at once available and so easily misjudged and overlooked, are to be found in experiences not requiring refined conceptualization, but in experiences readily shareable, that can be sung, imaged or written with an economy of means that, without banalizing them, raises them to a level of visibility, appreciability few poets have, perhaps, aspired even to attain.

RECOGNITION, EMBRACE

As Prévert writes in his intensely parodic "Souvenirs de famille" ("Family Memories") from *Paroles*, things change, a new life can begin, "somewhat different from the previous one, but always moon and sun alternating"(1,21). Such a fundamental constancy of what is, of the earth's givenness – and the constancy in change characteristically is made to appear funny, delightful, joy-bearing – we can, oddly enough, so easily overlook. Yet such constancy remains, for Prévert, one of the essential factors of our being which we need to recognise and, indeed, celebrate. Such recognition reinserts us psychically, emotionally, spiritually – again, the word I use without any religious connotations – in a world, a cosmos, whose mystery and exquisite innocence – water lapping the shore, the sun breaking through clouds, flowers opening, the wind rustling the leaves of trees in which nest stunningly fragile yet sturdy birds – we can vastly neglect in the midst of personal and social turmoil we fundamentally create and impose upon the earth. Recognition, certainly, does not obviate consciousness of what in "Pater noster", from *Paroles* (1,40-41), Prévert refers to as "the frightful misfortunes of the world / Which are legion / With their legionaries / With their torturers / With the masters of the world"; but, equally, it advocates we not blind ourselves in consequence of such consciousness, to "all the wonders of the world / Which are there / Simply upon the earth / Offered to everyone / scattered about / Marvelling themselves at being such wonders". One thinks of Novalis' similar perception of the earth's marvelousness, wonderfully present yet fragmented, scattered about the globe to a point of possible invisibility. In effect, Prévert's recognition involves a perception of the earth as, as he writes in "Chanson dans le sang" ("Song in the Blood"), still from *Paroles* – and we can see that such factors as concern us here are central from the outset to Prévert's poetics – involves a perception of the earth, then, as being royally transcendent of humanity's foibles and exaggerations. Blood may flow upon the earth, as the poem argues (1,67-8), but the earth "doesn't give a damn / it turns / it doesn't stop turning", just as war and blood do not stop, must not stop, the singing of the earth, the "song" of the earth. Bloodied it may be; but its deep constancies transcend such contradiction and, indeed, show repeatedly, endlessly, how much their recognition is fundamental to our self-transformation, a new recognition of ourselves as creatures of the earth.

This type of now explicit now implicit consciousness can frequently lead Prévert to dwell on the interconnectedness of the earth's phenomena. Witness the discreet and lovely throw-away poem from *Paroles*, "L'Automne" ("Autumn", 1,129):

> Un cheval s'écroule au milieu d'une allée
> Les feuilles tombent sur lui
> Notre amour frissonne
> Et le soleil aussi
> (A horse collapses in the middle of a riding-path
> The leaves fall down upon it
> Our love shivers
> As does the sun.)

This sensitivity to a kind of Gaia-like interwovenness of experiences and events across the face of the planet makes Prévert not just an ecologist well before his time, but a man continuing – without insistence, system, intellectualisation – a tradition of interlocking telluric consciousness not only Hugolian or Romantic but with roots in many of the world's great founding myths, Western, Oriental, Aboriginal, Inuit, and so on. Rather than dwell – it *is* a choice – on our alienation, Prévert suggests – implicitly only: he is not a moralist – that we remain alert to our telluric insertedness and thus our joinedness. Despite our, or others', pain and suffering, it remains feasible, as the close of "Place du Carrousel" ("Merry-go-round Square") indicates, to maintain that strangely transcendent "splendor and mystery of adversity / blood and glimmerings / beauty stricken / Fraternity"(1,148). That "gulf" of anguish to which we can be drawn, like the philosopher Prévert gently mocks in "La Tour"("The Tower") from *Spectacle* – "Sometimes an intelligent man / To escape a bee-sting / Plunges his entire head into the hive / Cursing the Queen" (1,248-9) – such anguish as we may experience can be dealt with more effectively by adopting the simple earthy wisdom of the same poem's washerwoman: "Life is beautiful when it's beautiful / And it often happens it is" (1,252).

In looking about himself, then, Prévert so commonly observes the wonderfully "public splendor of natural history"("Soleil de mars" ("March Sun"1,676)). Each day, he delightfully puts it at the end of the long "Intempéries" ("Bad Weather"), can thus become "the anniversary of the day" (1,787), an ongoing celebration of earth's revelation in time. All that is required is "keep[ing] wide open one's window overlooking the sea, the earth, life" ("Diurnes"

("Diurnals",2,53)). Yes, Prévert knows only too well, the earth is constantly vandalised, by city-dwellers he tells us in *Arbres* (2,151), by all those who mockingly pillage its manifold abundances – forests, lakes, rivers, its wildlife, its air, etc. –, not thinking that, as he writes in "À Cassis comme ailleurs" ("In Cassis as Elsewhere", 2,819), "one fine day, it will laugh right back at you". Yes, Prévert can muse as to the likelihood of the very survival of vegetal, even human life in the current climate of bare recognition of the kind of planetary, even cosmic interwovenness we have seen him evoke. And yes, when Prévert prepares to conclude his fine text on Alexander Calder (*Fêtes (Celebrations)*), he can speak of the artist as having "his feet on the ground and his head on his shoulders. But in this head spin three-ton stabiles, black alarm signals pointing to love endangered, red wine spilled, the earth threatened" (2,209). But, finally, Prévert equally knows, the earth is a book of profound mystery and vast resourcefulness, clearly much wiser than its human inhabitants often show themselves to be. As he wittily says in "Rouge" from *Choses et autres*, we don't leave behind so easily the earth, "that loving and generous mother-daughter who never, ever, knew her father" (2,356). Our "return" to earth is, thus, a necessity, an amusing/serious requirement that the recognition of earth be full and that our embrace of the latter be as generous and as loving as its of ourselves.

ANIMALS

Prévert's "defence and illustration" of the strange but certain beauties of the animals of the planet, at once wild and domesticated, is no doubt well enough known, especially by the children of France and, to some extent, the French-speaking world – who will have often read books such as *Le Petit Lion (The Lion Cub)*, *Des bêtes (Animals)*, *Lettre des îles Baladar (Letter from the Baladar Islands)*, or *Opéra de la lune (Moon Opera)*. If we look directly at a couple of poems published posthumously, "Éléphant..." (2,416-17) and "Âne dormant" ("Sleeping Donkey", 2,419-20), we can see a good deal that is pertinent to Prévert's fascination. The first of these texts stresses that the latter is not predicated upon what, one has to admit, would be rather fanciful notions of "respect" and "tenderness". This would be too sentimentally improbable for Prévert. No, what strikes him is the sheer natural beauty of the elephant, its "trueness", its livingness and the dignity of its being even when subjected to human control. The second text emphasizes the need simply to look at the donkey as it sleeps and dreams away. Prévert is even more sensitive here to the relative mistreatment inflicted by humans upon other animals. But he presses us:

> Regardez-le
> Il est plus beau que les statues qu'on vous dit
> d'admirer et qui vous ennuient.
> Il est vivant, il respire, confortablement installé
> dans son rêve.
> (Look at him
> He is more beautiful than the statues you're told to
> admire and which bore you.
> He's living, he's breathing, settled in the comfort
> of his dreaming.)

For Prévert, it is the sheer magnificent presence of such a creature that we need properly to get our minds around. Only such a marvelling appreciation can do justice to the donkey – and ourselves. And Prévert's delightful flourish in the second part of the poem about the donkey coming to the assistance of the little boy deemed a donkey, an ass, by his teacher, is crowned by his crucial insistence upon the consciousness and dream-life of all living creatures: "And if the donkey isn't dreaming that / It's because he's dreaming something else. / All we can know is he's dreaming. / Everyone dreams".

Birds, of course, play a significant role in the works of Prévert, not just in symbolic terms but also, as ever, for their sheer physical mystery: their immense power and stamina despite their seeming fragileness, their grace in flight, their collective sense and solidarity, their delight in the ordinary: air, water, light, the "humble" loci of the world (streets, fields, markets, slums and so on), etc. "Salut à l'oiseau" ("Hail to Birds", 1,143-5) from *Paroles* offers a wonderful concatenation of the endless "variety" of birds, their virtues, their frequentations. "Fairylike", naturally given to happiness, free, equal, fraternal – as any French person should be by definition! – birds for Prévert befriend children or madmen, the proletariat, bohemians, good-for-nothings, everyone and anyone and pretty well anywhere. To greet them is like greeting an ideal world population, unfussy, non-judgemental, merrily dynamic, unpretentious, simply happy to be alive. "Au hasard des oiseaux" ("As Birds Come and Go", 1,118-19), from the same collection, confirms this "exemplariness", which, as Prévert points out, has nothing to do with human moral or social niceties but everything to do with being, aliveness in its most uncluttered state:

> exemple des oiseaux
> exemples les plumes les ailes le vol des oiseaux
> exemple le nid les voyages et les chants des oiseaux
> exemple la beauté des oiseaux
> exemple le coeur des oiseaux
> la lumière des oiseaux
> (the example of birds
> e.g. feathers wings the flight of birds
> e.g. the nest the travellings and the song of birds
> e.g. the beauty of birds
> e.g. the hearts of birds
> the light of birds.)

The animals other than birds to which Prévert tends to draw our attention – for there is a choice: no poisonous snakes, no deadly spiders nor piranhas (although Prévert, one might guess, would have been inclined to stress their natural innocence and the mystery of their being) – are dogs, monkeys, cats, giraffes, llamas, penguins, seals, lions, cows, horses, camels, deer, sheep, pigs, zebras: those animals Ylla photographs for the 1950 book with Prévert. He knows well, of course, that the animal world is, as Woody Allen put it, one vast smorgasbord; but he knows too that animals – except for humans – do not kill out of cruelty or gratuitousness, lack of need. They do so, as he wittily puts it, "politely" (1,205), and, so often, are otherwise known for their "tenderness", their lack of "principles" and "mentalness" as *we* know them (cf. 1,181) – essentially a strong point in their favor for Prévert! Certainly, Prévert grants to animals a consciousness that, as he says in *Hebdromadaires* (2,908), many "thinkers" deny them. But it is clear that he deems it a much more ecologically attuned and tellurically sensitive consciousness than that usually demonstrated by humans, and one that he does not otherwise presume to conceptualize. What, most essentially, Prévert thus emphasizes is the need to look, with an open mind and a marvelling heart, upon the vast range of animal life around us. "Friends" so many of the world's creatures may be, but, he stresses, they remain "those unknown friends mysterious or charming/secret and formidable distant and stunning"(*Des bêtes,* 1,186). They are there, living, in the world, yet, like so many other phenomena (laughter, a kiss, song), deeply strange, wonderful but not reducible – and, as such, they are best evoked analogically, not in some definitorily absolute mode:

> Des bêtes
> comme des choses disparues et jamais oubliées
> comme une étoile filante une blessure un baiser
> comme un éclat de rire une source une chanson
> comme des feuilles sur les arbres
> des îles sous le vent
> des hommes dans les rues et d'autres en prison
> (Animals
> like things long-gone and never forgotten
> like a shooting star a wound a kiss
> like a burst of laughter a spring a song
> like leaves on the trees
> leeward islands
> men on the streets and others in gaol)

Prévert at his subtle and accessible best, always with darting flourishes that prod and reorient, such as the last line: animals as strange and infinitely (in)definable/(in)comparable as ordinary, nameless people and, even, those detained by those in a position to detain...

Which leads to a couple of final points. Prévert was never a vegetarian, but he did speak out on a good number of occasions against the modern conditions of breeding and raising animals for food – the widespread use of hormones and chemicals in forced feeding, etc. – and the manifest suffering and fear of animals in modern abattoirs (cf. "Irrespect humain" ("Human Disrespect", 2,224)). Hunting, shooting, trapping, leave him equally unimpressed, for today such activity is largely a "sport", a rather fatuous demonstration of one's (usually) manly "great[ness] in the face of Eternity". As Prévert says with typical punch and pertinence in "Folklore", "to the rear of Eternity a squirrel couldn't give a damn about my [greatness]"(2,928). And although zoos often allow us –

and Prévert, at times – to see those strange and beautiful creatures he invites us to look at, precisely to appreciate their extraordinary and mysterious exquisiteness, zoos remain, too, a place in which, as he writes in "La Belle Vie" ("The Beautiful Life") from *Spectacle*, the principle of animal fraternity has been betrayed (1,334). As the cooped and caged animals say to one another, "the world has kicked us out [of real life] / Life has buggered us up completely" (1,334). In the final analysis the freedom of all creatures remains, ethically, at the center of Prévert's stance here: a principle of gentle, unabusive anarchy. The celebrated "Pour faire le portrait d'un oiseau" ("How to Paint a Bird", 1,106-7), from *Paroles*, turns essentially on the principle of freedom and coexistence. To paint a bird – to interact with any non-human animal – demands, of the human animal, respect, appreciation and a commitment to liberation, to non-exploitation.

TREES

The poem, from *Spectacle*, titled "La Guerre" ("War",1,271) is not really a poem about trees, even though they remain metaphorically central. "You're deforesting / you fools / you're deforesting", the poem begins, "all the young trees with the old axe / you're taking out". Prévert's poem, of course, is written against the wholesale destruction of France's youth by morally righteous leaders prepared to sacrifice it in the name of "right and wrong / ... Victory / ... Freedom". The "old trees with their old roots / their old false teeth" remain unaffected, content with their military parading... But, if trees here are pure emblems, they do remain emblems of life, of growth, of strange and beautiful natural energy, and the poem does theatricize the tensions of innocent, unrestricted vitality and belief-systems that frustrate and disregard this vitality. In their natural state, all trees – like all humans – simply grow, beyond hierarchy and imprisoning, (self-)abusive concept.

The trees of London that Prévert speaks of in his *Charmes de Londres* are, like so many animals Prévert evokes, like the "young trees" depicted in "La Guerre", far from ideally placed, ecologically, in relation to the earth's imaginable edenic perfection. "Great trees of London", Prévert apostrophizes, "like the last buffalo you are relegated / far far behind the iron railings / of your great parks and public gardens" (1,500). Yet, though under threat, under human pressure, such trees still are perceived as "oas[es] of coolness and light", places of laughter and ease, placed where the love of children can be straightforwardly, unintellectually, reciprocated. "London Trees / masterpieces", Prévert concludes with such light-fingered and joyous insight, "of the old Forestry and Environment Commission museum". Today we think of the disappearing rain forests. Prévert thinks back, rather, to when England was almost completely wooded, from top to bottom, side to side.

Of course, of all the texts in which Prévert shows his fascination with and admiration for trees, the wonderful 1967 book prepared in collaboration with Ribemont-Dessaignes – though Prévert wrote certain parts even ten years earlier – is undoubtedly the most memorable. *Arbres*, a book of some twenty-six pages (2,133-59) and some fourteen constituent parts, opens as follows:

> arbres
> > chevaux sauvages et sages
> à la crinière verte
> au grand galop discret
> > dans le vent vous piaffez
> debout dans le soleil vous dormez
> > et rêvez
> Et le dessinateur
> > le chasseur de bonheur
> > sans vous faire aucun mal
> vous tire le portrait
> > et vous vous réveillez
> > et vous le laissez faire
> > et même vous l'aidez
> modèles exemplaires
> > et désintéressés
> (trees
> > wild and wise horses
> green-maned
> galloping along discreetly
> > in the wind you prance and toss
> in the sun you sleep standing up
> > and dream away
> And the person sketching
> > the happiness hunter

                    without hurting you in any way
              fires off your portrait
                          and you wake up
                          and let him go about things
                          and even help him
                    exemplary and disinterested
                          models)

Trees, then, initially – though not quite initially, for, after an
opening, capitalized "Trees" echoing the title, monolithic, generic,
all-embracing, there appears in the text one of Ribemont-Dessaignes'
discreetly powerful engravings – trees, then, after the artist has *shown*
them to us in his very beautiful manner, are represented by Prévert
analogically. We thus at once delight in the sideways, playful dance
of the tree-horse metaphor and understand to what degree, if we
really think about it, as *Arbres* intends us to, trees *are* indefinable –
except as what they are not: namely, language. If they are "wild and
wise", it is because Prévert deems them so, just as he can deem them
to be "horses". Their freedom, their untamedness, are not constrained
by Prévert's terms, because, clearly, he is playing with them via his
own expressive means. Similarly, the trees' wisdom or good behavior
is not predicated on negative self-constraint, but rather a self-
discipline or, again, self-definition or self-expression, an idea Prévert
himself merely *plays* with. The idea, too, that trees – like donkeys –
dream and awaken to some other level of consciousness, can only be
intuitive, joyfully, playfully so, though it clearly is deeply felt by a
man for whom all life and all life-forms remain a profound and
(largely) magnificent mystery we, as humans, so greatly neglect or
radically undervalue. The human relation, of the artist, to the tree –
which the second stanza elaborates, basically echoes the message of
"Pour faire le portrait d'un oiseau": human exchange is always most
productive if it is respectful of difference, gentle, joy-seeking,
centered on being, co-being, and not raw having, domination,
exploitation.

　　　　Equality and even equivalence, depite difference, of tree and
human: a powerful, provocative, yet also happily ludic statement
about (our) being-in-the-world... Life is life, no matter what odd and
delightfully distinct form it may take. Trees thus – again, seriously
and playfully: this only can be the truly wise mode of articulation and
definition – trees thus have a pedigree (cf. 2,138), as long as any

human's and their language, their mode of (self-)expression, is veritably ancient and particular. "Trees speak tree / the way children speak child" (2,135). If Prévert's poetics does not converge in many respects with that of Francis Ponge, there certainly is some important affinity here in the recognition of the divergence of the language of things and that of human beings, and yet the logic of what Ponge deems to be the latter's differential-cum-analogical mode of relating to the real.

In preference to intellectualizing such rapidly intuited and poetically integrated thoughts, however, Prévert tends in *Arbres,* as so often elsewhere, to stress either the plainly positive aspects of the life of trees, of the dimensions of the latter which may give us pause. In both cases, he tends to surprise or provoke; nothing is as predictable as we might have imagined it would be. Thus trees are magical, "abracadabrarbre[s]" he untranslatably puts it (2,141); they are loci of melody, classical or minimalist, "arias of woods and forests" (2,140), or, in cities, "in this beggarly street / totally severe and widowy / a little strain of unusual / salutary green / music" (2,150). Thus, equally, but storming off in the opposite but not really at all opposite (: these are still trees) direction, Prévert can remind us how trees have been transformed/deformed/reformed into flagpoles, prison cages, scaffolding, gibbets, picture frames, violins, coach wheels, handles, and the list goes on, stirring up its mixed emotions and its heightened consciousness of human psychology, whilst ever reminding us of the strange, serene adaptability of our coinhabitants of the world, trees themselves. For, if Prévert remains sensitive to the way in which tree-human relations have been distorted – "before lumberjacks / had regard for trees / before lumberjacks / drank to their health / before lumberjacks / used to sing" (2,155) – this erosion of the sense of the earth's mysterious sacredness precisely allows him to press upon us the beauty and urgency of the latter. To recover that sense could assist us, Prévert feels, in reestablishing a lost equilibrium, in regaining the love, the happiness, the wisdom that, intrinsically, dwells within trees (cf. 2,146-7).

OTHER THINGS

Trees may occupy a somwhat privileged place in Prévert's writings, but, as we can readily understand, their "meaning and their

logic" apply broadly to the natural world at large and all of its
teeming "things". "Soleil de mars" (1,676) from *La Pluie et le beau
temps* begins as follows:

> Oranges des orangers
> citrons des citronniers
> olives des oliviers
> ronces des ronceraies
> Mystères fastueux et journaliers
> (Oranges of orange trees
> lemons of lemon trees
> olives of olive trees
> brambles of bramble patches
> Showy and everday mysteries)

Prévert is, of course, not the only poet of his day to be affected
profoundly by the splendid and enigmatic presence of things: one
thinks of contemporaries such as Char and Guillevic, Bonnefoy and
Jaccottet, and younger poets can readily share Prévert's admiration:
Marie-Claire Bancquart or Yves Leclair, Denise Le Dantec or
Jeannine Baude. What is relatively particular to Prévert, however, is
an uninhibited insistence upon factors of love and joy, beauty and
mystery in his evocation of the "things" of the world; a general
resistance to their intellectualized conceptualization; a consequent
desire to speak to the simple heart rather than the cluttering mind, to
the child in the adult, to the ordinary man or woman in the bourgeois;
an edge, nevertheless, that is politically and socially rebellious – or,
better, unaccepting of dogma and standard belief.

Indeed, what Prévert often likes in things, natural or
domesticated – knives, forks, spoons, for example, as in the ever
delightfully witty "Un homme et un chien" ("A Man and a Dog",
1,348) from *Spectacle* – is, despite their love and fraternalness, the
serene disregard they happily display with respect to the often absurd
belief systems that swarm and proliferate around and through them.
Fatras can speak in the poem so titled (2,105-6) of "the secret
celebration" (*la fête secrète)* of the world's fantastic array of
"objects" that can be found in any small space, a celebration Prévert
fully understands as intrinsic to things, to materiality, a state of being
we might, with Prévert, sense, though not comprehend. Moreover,
there is no hint here of the nausea at the sight of the strangeness of

things Sartre can attribute to his anti-hero – even though he confessed, to Simone de Beauvoir, to never having experienced such nausea himself. No, in Prévert, if "the ugliest of fleas is someone", and "the least grain of sand is full size"("Diurnes", 2,43), it is their splendid enigmaticalness and their unrelatedness to humanity's scales and measures that are elating (cf. 2,43). To see the things that proliferate around and with us, large or small, demands openness, as does their evaluation, their appreciation. Seeing is a trickier art than one might have imagined, as "Graffiti", from *Grand Bal du printemps* makes clear: "Even if you don't / look upon it too kindly / the landscape is / not ugly / it's your eye / that / perhaps is off" (1,441). Life's "things" need embracing fully, unconditionally, the opening poem of *Fatras* tells us: "Bring in the dog covered in mud / Too bad for those who don't like either dogs or mud" ("Tant pis" ("Too bad", 2, 3)): the world is a remarkable place, its "things" are always to be "remarked", they are always "clean", despite appearances, always gathering into "miraculous" convergence, magnetized order – just like the coming together, in the marvellously funny poem from *Histoires et autres histoires*, "Comme par miracle" ("As if by Miracle", 1,841-2), of a man and his wife, an orange peel and a passing priest.

The "things" of nature in general have, of course, a special place in Prévert's writing and heart, "rivers, woods and meadows", for example, in "Aubervilliers" (1,336), which can become the objects of "the simple dreams of workmen", workmen, and indeed working women, so often in their industrial urban lives cut off, or so it seems, from a fulfilment of such dreams. The sea, at Pornichet, the sixty-nine year-old Prévert conjures up from his early childhood with vibrant passion: it had the power, the power of nature's mysterious and free things, to "change people", to reintroduce them to their own still available naturalness, a profound "otherness" dwelling latently within them ("Enfance", 2,228). Things, certainly, can be appreciated, humanized, shifted from their inherent unspeakableness. Prévert himself can describe the river Seine, in the fine "La Seine a rencontré Paris" ("The Seine has met up with Paris"), as "scabrous dangerous tumultuous and dreamy into the bargain / That's how she is / Mischief caress romance tenderness caprice / Dirty tricks laziness" (2,343). But, of course, in picturing the Seine as a place of multifariousness and contradiction, Prévert opens it up once more to its indescribable mystery. Like Char's river Sorgue, bubbling through Provence, the Seine's waters may front upon much that is human, but they spring and flow forth in "secret celebration" of their phenomenality, their amazing natural presence. Like the fruit and eggs Prévert evokes in *Arbres*, the Seine remains "inexplicable / unexplained" (2,142). As inexplicable "as the dizziness of lovers / as the beauty of almond trees" (2,142).

Which, let us emphasize, does clearly not mean that things are unknowable, but merely – yet so essentially for Prévert – that our human characterizations, equations and definitions are so often not quite – or at all – to the point. A truer "equation" might gather rather the strands of that sense of beauty, and abiding strangeness, which a "simple", "dreaming", unintellectualized approach to the world's things can maintain. If we take a few samplings of the many poems where Prévert speaks of flowers, for example, we can see that the "value" and "meaning" of flowers demand equations and definitions which neither our information-technology-based approaches nor our more classically conceptualizing analyses come close to creating. What fascinates Prévert in these "things", is their sheer livingness and the ineffable qualities – the yellowness, shiningness, of the helianthus, for example – they display (cf. "Fleurs et couronnes" ("Flowers and Crowns", 1,44)). Or, elsewhere, in "Maraîchers d'avant guerres" ("Prewars Market Gardeners", 1,449), Prévert looks back – but, we feel, implicitly forward too – to times when wars did not/do not, in their aftermath, politicize flowers at the otherwise simple, working person's *fête du travail*, imposing upon lilies of the vally or sweetbriar, "priceless beneath the rain", values, patriotic though they may be, utterly foreign to their intrinsic mystery and beauty. "La Fleur" ("The Flower", 2,347), from *Choses et autres*, thus makes abundantly clear that a flower is priceless, inestimable in its worth, because it is free, authentic, "useful as bread / useful as wine" – lifegiving, in effect – , rebellious to all we may seek to exploit it for, wonderfully available, "the flower of anyone when anyone is someone / the flower of brilliant colors bursting forth anywhere when anywhere is everwhere / bursting with life / bursting with laughter" – but, Prévert adds, for this emblematic flower is ever menaced, "with anxiety / and distress too". The poem "En passant" ("Walking By", 1,495), from *Charmes de Londres*, at once confirms this vulnerability – "the [whole] vegetable kingdom [is] threatened today", Prévert will remark a few pages further on (1,501) – and yet insists on the exquisite, unmetaphorical floralness of all that is innocent, youthful, unaffected by forces that unfree, render inauthentic, disfigure, exploit: "Why say resembles // Just as in these crates all the fruit is fruit / this child is a flower / a flower of life". If all things beautiful, sublimely, delicately free and unspoiled, are intrinsically flowers, it is because for Prévert the flower radiates that exquisite and mysterious, unspeakable pure "thingness" that humans don't always realise lies richly latent within themselves. The flower is their sign; the sign of an unclutteredness, an ineffableness they can live, remember, become again, if all pretensions to being other than this joyous florality are dropped. To become the flower we are is to assume our phenomenality, our phenomenalness.

STREETS

Prévert has always been a lover of the streets of the earth. In that, he is not alone, of course. Jacques Réda, today, or, not long ago, Aragon (*Le Paysan de Paris (Paris Peasant)*) or Léon-Paul Fargue (*Le Piéton de Paris (Paris Pedestrian)*) speak, like Prévert, of the "fairytale quality of the streets" (1,892), the magic they deploy in the midst of their apparent ordinariness, the fact that it is there, at the heart of their strangely ever available theatrical space, that "the true Museum of Man" can be found, "even though this label, with its vintage misogyny guaranteed, invites laughter"(CF. "Rouge", 2,355). Streets, with their buzz and hum are the sign, for Prévert, writing at the close of this same poem, that "nothing is lost", that if "red misfortune" can rear up, it can also be "erased, red happiness mak[ing] its entrance". Streets are thus wonderfully spontaneous, creative, alive, shifting spaces of freedom and possibility, wherein the marvellous can spring improbably forth, wherein, moreover, anonymity is, delightfully, king or queen.

No wonder Prévert's mind so frequently goes back to the streets of Paris or Toulon, Harlem, New York, or the country roads around Pornichet, in telling the tale of his childhood ("Enfance", 2,215-53). Walking, as "Chanson des escargots qui vont à l'enterrement" ("Song of the Snails going to a Funeral", 1,51) affirms, is a way of "seeing something of the world"; it lets us traverse frontiers, perceive difference, live the bizarre mosaical connectedness of the things and creatures of the earth. Prévert's Tom Thumb, in the first text, "L'Autruche" ("The Ostrich"), of *Contes pour enfants pas sages* (1,861), skips off merrily from parental guidance to discover the world for himself. Holiday in Pornichet, near La Baule, is spent tramping the lanes, roads and paths of the area: such activity *is*, essentially, the holiday (2,229). The great film made with Carné – to which I shall return in the next-but-one chapter – ends with the magnificent scene of the swarming, festive flow of people down those great open, open-ended, public boulevards of Paris, a scene not unlike that painted of Paris in 1906 at the beginning of "Enfance", where the streets are the place of a teeming infinity, multiplicity and dynamism attaching to human life (2,215-16).

To walk the streets, to jump on the back of trams or passing trucks to go further afield – "Enfance" (2,247) is a wonderful source – or to reach those vast open green streets, called parks (cf. 2,247), where walking, running and playing merge and are always synonymous with liberty, discovery of self and other, harmony with the earth, the sky, our animality plunged into vegetation and light, with the wind upon one's face and blowing through one's mind – such experience remains, unsurprisingly, ever central to Prévert's writing, its meaning, its purpose. For streets, parks, the wind – none of these are intellectual metaphors in Prévert, even though they may carry an emblematic force vaster than themselves. The wind which Prévert evokes at the close of his powerful "Sainte âme"("Holy Soul",2,22) from *Fatras*, is thus a fundamental and *lived* element amongst the elements of the earth. "With it I shall travel", Prévert declares. Travel, free, primary, mysterious and dynamic breath of life, down the streets and roads of cities and villages, across the open spaces of parks, wasteland or sea, into the bodies and psyches of the world, through the walls that separate, joyously, playfully transgressing the limits we impose upon ourselves...

> ... regarde / ... / ... / avec tendresse détresse et amitié / avec ardente lucidité
> (... look / ... / ... / with tenderness distress and friendship / with burning lucidity)
> Jacques Prévert, "La Couleur de la lumière" ("The Color of Light", 2,533)

PICASSO

If Prévert's writings on art are, in addition to his collaborations, numerous and diversified, certain artists draw his particular attention. Picasso is amongst these artists and as the 1940 poem from *Paroles,* "Lanterne magique de Picasso" ("Picasso's Magic Lantern", 1,152-7), shows, Prévert's admiration stems in significant measure from the teeming, ever changing transmutations, juxtapositions and imaginative choices Picasso's work reveals. Everything speaks of energy, desire, intensity; everything is discovery and revelation, "real and surreal / terrifying and funny"; everything created constitutes and refounds a world at once "indisputable and unexplained", where the quotidian merges with the strange, but where beauty reigns amidst "the puzzle of love with all its bits and pieces". The prose poem of 1944, "Eaux-fortes de Picasso" ("Picasso's Etchings"), opts for a quite different angle of approach, inasmuch as Prévert's intentions seem at first to be descriptive (of Picasso's work devoted to the Minotaur myth, with its interlaced themes of love and death) and gently, unmoralisingly playful – the Minotaur "caresses, with his divine bovine eye, and not thinking about anything, all the secret gardens of the magnificent cocottes who offer themselves so simply and so naturally to him" (*Spectacle*, 1,368). If the tone is somewhat vaudevillesque as Danièle Gasiglia-Laster has suggested, it is subtly so, and – it is Prévert's second intention here – seeks neither to disrupt Picasso's creative inventiveness nor to forego the opportunity, via this joint play, to prod and poke away in characteristic Prévertian fashion at human cruelty, moral pretentiousness or plain foolishness. The text finishes, however, by returning us to Picasso's own genial tactics: art as compassionate, "fraternal caress" of the marginal, the "exiled", the "monstruous"; art as serene transcendence of received idea and form, as a "shaking off of the fleas [of all of mythology's myths]"; art as a *mise à mort* of the pre-existing, a radical appropriation and rewriting thereof.

Two other texts demonstrate the inalienable sense of affinity Prévert felt with Picasso's teeming, spontaneous creativity: "Diurnes" from *Fatras* and *Portraits de Picasso (Portraits of Picasso)*. The first of these two appeared in 1962 as a single volume, with thirty photographic "interpretations" by André Villers of cutouts and overlays realised by Picasso (2,43-54). As ever, Prévert's text is shimmering and alive, unpredictable yet focused, rooted in the genial collaborations before his eyes yet complementing them in Prévert's own darting, shiningly enthused creative play. Here, Prévert sees Picasso's exceptional energy in various significant ways. Firstly Picasso's own "naturalness" is that of nature itself. What we might term "disfiguration" or "figuration" or "transfiguration" (cf. 2,45) is but the ever-shifting mode of creation / the Creation. Naturally, "la nature ne lui en tient pas rigueur" ("nature doesn't hold it against him", 2,45). Picasso is merely "un enfant naturel" (2,45), an illegitimate son as natural as the day is long. Secondly, all the enchanting forms and figures of Picasso's *découpages* – brilliantly photographed by Villers and enhanced by further ensuing collaboration initiated by Picasso based on the initial photographing – are signs of the artist's creative aliveness, of Picasso's endless creativity "Here and Now", ever "allergic to despair as much as to melancholy" (cf. 2,45). Such forms are thus, thirdly – as one of them is made to say in Prévert's wonderful imagined dialogue of the "goblins" Picasso has conjured – signs of our ever possible being. "No doubt I am he who can be", the dialogue begins. "Perhaps I am he who has no doubt about it", is the rejoinder (2,46). Picasso is thus seen by Prévert – it is his fourth insight – to be playing a game called "Le Désir attrapé par la queue" ("Desire caught by the tail", 2,49), for creation is the pursuit of the individual's desire and its momentary coincidence with its fulfilment. Finally – it is Picasso's Goat that Prévert has announce it – Picasso is an artist who, "wherever his place of dwelling is, keeps wide open his window giving on to the sea, the earth, life" (2,53). He is, in short, ever available, ever ready to gaze out upon what is. But, Picasso's seeing is not merely absorptive. Transmutation according to his desire is what is essential. "All landscapes he sees and, hands in his pockets, pleasing himself, ... he modifies them all" (2,53).

Portraits de Picasso (2,539-52) had already appeared, in Milan, in 1959, with photographs of Picasso and his working and living environment by André Villers. Allow me to stress just four points that, in the midst of this once again modally varied text, add to our sense of Prévert's appreciation of Picasso's genius. First, Picasso, in his own swarming ease and spontaneity, is participating in what Prévert sees as nature's ceaseless efforts "to do its own self-portrait" (2,539): what Picasso's work demonstrates is the capacity of being to explore itself endlessly. Second, in Prévert's amusingly imagined radio show, Picasso is understood as not concerned with theorising, with purely abstract (self-)definition, but with experiencing being, desiring and participating in it, self-creating and co-creating with its endlessly malleable substance (cf. 2,543). Third, always, and fundamentally, Picasso is "a painter of love" (2,551). Finally – and in consequence of this love of what is, what can be, this love of the created and the endlessly creatable – Picasso's work is an offering to the world, it installs itself back in the world, nature, the cosmos, its place of (self-)"exhibition" is "the museum of the sun, the moon and the elements" (2,252).

MIRÓ

Prévert's writings on and for Miró are quite numerous: nine pieces in total. "Enfance à Tarragone" ("Tarragona Childhood", 2,512-13) centers initially upon Miró's characteristically strong and evocative use of color, red and black in particular here, thinking perhaps of the 1945 painting *La Course de taureaux (Bull Running)*. Quickly however, this free verse poem shifts its focus to the young Miró's intuitive exchange with the strangeness of life's phenomena as they manifest themselves in the full and deep minimalities of time, as Prévert sees it. Poems such as "Orage" ("Storm", 2,513-14) and "Oasis Miró" ("Miró Oasis", 2,514-15) clearly are inspired by paintings, often more than one, from the same period. If Prévert perceives tensions in Miró's thematics, symbols and colors – Prévert can speak, in "Romancero Miró" (2,516-24), of "the despairing metaphors of the avid poem of death / [that] punctuate the stanzas of suffering / anguish and ennui" in Miró's work –, he is equally alert to the implicit or explicit pursuit of that element that Reverdy similarly observes in Matisse's painterly gesture: "happiness [, stifled and drowned, ricocheting]".[1] This latter pursuit is fostered, Prévert suggests – in yet another poem devoted to Miró: "Astre âme drame" ("Star Soul Drama", 2,515-16) – by the artist's active response to the invitation things constantly throw out to him. "Call me Sesame / ask me to open up / the stone says to him // Miró does what it says", Prévert amusingly begins this latter poem. And, if he concludes by wittily remarking that "there is a mirror in Miró's name", we should certainly understand that it is a richly transformative mirror, yet, most importantly, like Stendhal's mirror held up to the world, one in contact with the real and thus far from gratuitously esoteric. As "Romancero Miró" puts it, already as a child Miró was "tracing out in his dream state / with a sure trembling and lucid finger / the map of the fabulous decors / of life's wild opera" (2,517). No hermeticism, but rather a rich symbiosis of self and other, inner and outer worlds. The same poem, as we have seen before, ends by pointing to the life-affirming, self-affirming relational structure that Miró's work thus develops through its endless "wanderings" and "dreamings". "Miró loves life / life loves Miró / life loves love / it's elementary" (2,524). When, moreover, Prévert writes in his "Cirque Miró" ("Miró's Circus", 2,525-6) – a powerful theme in Prévert as well as in Miró – that Miró is

> le jongleur le moins abstrait *in the world*
> (the least abstract juggler *in the world*),

Prévert is not just correcting certain impressions that can proliferate and *uproot* Miró's work from that earthy, visceral experience it in fact conveys, but, in all likelihood, is thinking of Baudelaire's famous – and ironic – invitation to catapult oneself "Any Where Out of the World" (*Le Spleen de Paris (Paris Spleen), XLVIII*). (If Baudelaire's poetics is arguably, in typical Symbolist fashion, one of spiritual flight

---

[1] See Reverdy's essay on Matisse in *Note éternelle du présent,* Flammarion, 1973.

from the world, it remains true that his entire oeuvre is caught up in an embrace of the latter – a love, if one likes, soured, anguished, ever frustrated, but real.)

One of Prévert's perhaps best known texts on Miró, titled "Aux jardins de Miró" ("In Miró's Gardens", 1,370-73), appeared for the first time in 1950 in the art and literature review *Derrière le miroir* and was taken up again for the major 1951 collection, *Spectacle*, itself in press five years after the first edition of *Paroles*. As ever, Prévert's phrasing is clever, playful, full of puns and linguistic elasticity and sheer inventiveness. The poem, too, cascades with satirical flourishes about the art world and its critics. Nothing unpleasant – as René Gilson rightly says, Prévert was not a "slandering man" in any way – but ever witty, or simply funny, occasionally provocative. And in the midst of it all – and with some quick digs at colonial attitudes – Miró becomes a black, a colored "brother of colors", free, "smiling and innocent / ... / in the garden of your dreams". Prévert's text, indeed, is never still, it never settles into some predictable pattern of thought, it is delightfully darting and busy in its expression and its meaning. And the poet reminds us finally of two crucial factors in our appreciation of the artist: 1. if art always goes towards the world, embracing and loving its teeming mysteries and wonders, if it thus "describes something / [, the artist] always paints at the same his or her own portrait": to paint the world is to paint oneself, and to look at Miró's work is to observe this double portrayal; 2. the work of art is always close to us all, if we can see with the eyes of children, with, here, the eyes of Prévert's little daughter, who tells her father before falling asleep: "my eyes are full of birds / surely I'm going to dream of a garden".

In 1956, Prévert published with the prestigious art publisher/gallery, Maeght, what is undoubtedly his most telling text on Miró, the book *Joan Miró* (2,506-12), with many reproductions of the artist's work and a second text by Georges Ribemont-Dessaignes, an artist also much admired by Prévert. The text opens in typical Prévertian fashion, it is punchy, with quick formulations, quite surprising in their veiled allusiveness, yet essentially unproblematic in what is, we realise, their determination to stick close to the subject at hand, Miró's life and work:

1917

Déjà chez l'usurier Charlot a mis depuis longtemps sa
montre à l'heure d'apres le calendrier

Sang du Dragon
arbre des Iles Fortunées

Un peu plus loin en Catalogne
les ciseaux des oiseaux ont découpé le temps

Petits morceaux immenses intenses et frémissants du grand
jeu de patience de l'amour et du vent

Sardane

Rêves mis en flacon
magie multicolore
humour du hérisson

Sardane

Assise une fille de ferme avec un plat de cerises sur son
tablier blanc

(1917

Already at the pawnbroker's Chaplin has long since put
his watch right according to the calendar

Dragon blood
tree of the Islands of the Blest

A bit further on in Catalonia
the birds' scissors have snipped out time

Little immense intense and quivering pieces of the great
game of patience of love and wind

Sardana

Bottled dreams
multicolored magic

humor of the bottle-brush hedgehog

Sardana

A farm girl sitting with a dish of cherries on her white apron)

Thus does Prévert rapidly evoke essential elements both of Miró's private life and his determining Catalan culture, and this via improbable yet elliptically pointed references (for example, to Charlie Chaplin's famous gesture in *The Pawnshop*: a situating of things [the film had come out in 1916, "already"], and an allusion to Miró's forced employment at seventeen in a very routine job, and, implicitly perhaps, his discovery of the "calendar" of the seasons in Montroig, where Miró convalesced and resumed painting; or to the centuries-old dragon tree of Tenerife: a tree oozing red sap, a place of predilection for the painter; or to the ancient Catalan solar dance, the sardana: Miró's fascination with the sun and his feeling of affinity to Catalan tradition) and by means of characteristic wordplay. This overture then glides smoothly – as the last line quoted shows – into very simple and admiring descriptions of paintings reproduced in *Joan Miró*. As for the lessons to be learned from Miró's work, we can sum up Prévert's insights as follows: 1. Miró's childhood is a time of passion, "outcrying", "violence" even, but it is precisely such a situation that pushes him towards self-liberation – moreover, both poet and painter realise that dream is already freedom and a great multiplier of presence, changing solitariness into a teeming "crowd"; 2. the "secrets" of things are penetrable via experience rather than through theory; 3. the sardana is the sign of Miró's sensitivity both to diurnal, telluric rhythm and to the vaster rhythm of the cosmos; 4. Miró's aesthetics is one of a fond enfolding: "Embrace and then embrace / embrace and rekindle / ever painting love / imaginary and true" (2,510): it is the love in the painterly embrace that gives truth to imagination; 5. Miró's creation is as fleshily, viscerally alert as it is imaginative: no real difference is maintained in his celebration of world and the self's "weddedness" to the world; 6. it is via a living of contrast, via a full acceptance of differences and changing moods and modes, that Miró can become the great artist he is: alternately solemn and smiling, delighted and amazed, "wise [and] wild", Miró flits from "grief" to "hope", problem to splendor, threat to reassurance, ever caught between a sense of life's flagrancy and its mystery.

CALDER

In 1971 Prévert publishes *Fêtes* (1,199-211), his one major text on the great American artist, Alexander Calder, almost an exact contemporary of the poet. (The opening part only had appeared in *Derrière le miroir* five years earlier.) Seven etchings by Calder illustrate Prévert's largely prose text, though Prévert by no means limits himself to a treatment of these alone, and, moreover, is quick to distance himself from any purely intellectualising critical approach: "thinking of him I am like those Gold Coast natives Jane Rouch speaks of... who say: 'To know is a pleasure but not to know is a joy'". As Danièle Gasiglia-Laster rightly points out (2,1073), what at bottom delights Prévert in Calder is his unclassifiableness, his natural, unforced defiance of category, and, in this, of course, he resembles – without at all resembling – Picasso and Miró. Pure freedom thus seems to be a principle at work in Calder's gesture; it makes his originality and the strange impression one can have of, as Prévert argues with perceptive flippancy, Calder's work being "as mysterious as anything". The sheer simplicity of Calder's creations – whether vast or small, whether we are looking at his mobiles or his "stabiles" or the etchings given in *Fêtes* – constantly strikes Prévert who, yet, understands instinctively the great, spontaneously articulated complexities that underpin a simplicity that Prévert doesn't hesitate to associate with the swirling and free imaginative impulse of "primitive" art and "childish truths". Moreover, as with other artists admired by Prévert – and, of course, so much of his global appreciation permits a direct entry into the most salient elements of his own aesthetics/ethics –, Calder is seen to be a "sorcerer... of happiness": his "work" becomes "pleasure", both in its process and as a product, a "pleasure of eyes and heart"; and, again, we can observe the absence of insistence upon intellectuality, pure rationality, a privileging rather of instinct, intuition, bodily and emotional intelligence. As with Miró and Picasso, the range of tone and sentiment is considerable. "Jovial engineer / Disturbing architect", Prévert calls Calder in his opening verse gambit, and he is quick to evoke both the charm and the "cruelty", the fairylike qualities and the "monstrousness" at work in Calder. Beauty, "embellish[ment of the world's] house", pleasure-seeking and pleasure-giving are at the center of what is urgent and purposeful in Calder. When, as Prévert writes, people ask the artist "what is its use, or what does it mean, the great anteater just smiles": charm, beauty, happiness, free self-expression are sufficient unto themselves, what superior "meaning" could one want? In this way Prévert prefers to see Calder as a supreme artisan or craftsman rather than someone given to artisticalness, a notion Prévert fights shy of, for it seems to him to smack of somewhat effete aestheticism – a workmanship too far from matter, the earth, the natural vigor of perfectly natural imaginative activity. The descriptions of Calder that tumble and twirl from Prévert's pen could take their place in the same magical circus the poet sees the artist's creations constantly performing: "fairy-fingered ogre"; "as simple as good-day when good-day is said for good – which is rare"; "Calder looks joyously like the little Bacchus sitting on his turtle, in Florence, in the Boboli gardens"; "a metallurgotechnician of *joie de vivre* in black and in color"; "if he's got his feet on the ground, it's only because he was born here"; "Calder is like that bear [who, once, in Biarritz, clipped me]. Now and then, he gives art a good clip of his paw, but to give it a helping hand, to put it on the right track"; and whilst "infernal and celestial machines can tirelessly reach for perfection, like Don Quixote's, Calder's mills carry on turning".

HENRIQUEZ

Prévert's earliest formal recognition of Elsa Henriquez' artistic talent comes in 1943, when for the catalogue of the Monaco exhibition introducing the very young painter's work, he offers both his celebrated poem, "Pour faire le portrait d'un oiseau" (1,106), and a short text of presentation, in the usual inimitable Prévertian style (2,481-2). Prévert's own poem, it is important to understand, is inspired by a series of twenty-eight pictures created by Henriquez and his presentational text focuses on qualities of discretion, non-self-centeredness and natural wonder before the world, qualities in the artist Prévert suggests we all can become: "In amazement in the face of beings and things [Elsa Henriquez] simply paints them". Prévert's text also maintains that Henriquez works – looks, sees and paints – in utter innocence, in this way projecting as it were innocence onto all that is either "tender" or "cruel", giving a childlike aura to her tiny created worlds that are "at once reasonable and wacky".

Subsequently, Prévert and Henriquez – daughter of the Peruvian dancer Helba Huara and the French painter-photographer Emile Savitry, to both of whom Prévert will offer praise and recognition – will collaborate in the production, notably, of the 1947 *Contes pour enfants pas sages* (1,901-66) and the 1952 *Guignol* (1,555-73). Later, in 1954, the artist will create thirty illustrations for what was the second poem of *Paroles*, "Histoire du cheval" ("Tale of the Horse", 1,12-14). Speaking of this "tale", but also of others, Maurice Blanchot stresses how each "is narrated in a mode that disarticulates it, making it impossible or imposing it as a magnificent hoax" (cf. 1,1019). And, of course, if this is true of Prévert's imaginative projections, as it may indeed be said to be, Prévert himself appreciates how it equally pertains to Henriquez' "narrativity". The text of the above 1947 collaboration is, moreover, taken up in the 1963 *Histoires et autres histoires* (1,859-73), with, as for the "Pour faire le portrait d'un oiseau"(1,106), a dedication to Elsa Henriquez. Neither it nor *Guignol* are intended, of course, to comment on the work of the artist, but the discourse is implicit: Henriquez has fresh, genial imagination, uncluttered by current aesthetic fashion or theory; her gesture dips into the natural createdness of "beings and things" and honors the innocence and simplicity of her own creative impulse.

These are no small merits in the eyes of Prévert. A final presentational *plaquette* for Elsa Henriquez' 1959 Paris exhibition makes clear the poet's admiration (2,553-4). In a typically witty, barely translatable manner, Prévert provocatively pushes aside academic niceties, arguing implicitly the imbrication, the equivalence even, of the real and the imaginative; the central force of love in creativity; the foolishness of thinking for a moment that Henriquez' work is "apainting": painting is painting is painting, as Americans say, and as Prévert ceasely argues – it's not complicated! "She is not there to resolve issues", Prévert writes, "she's there to paint and it's all very well for ideas to be in the air, their metaphysical fallout can't touch her". In short, Henriquez paints the things of her/the world. Prévert's text concludes, smilingly, caressingly, with his unique quirky grace:

Et si elle peint un Indien c'est pareil. Il
est à cheval devant la cordillère dans la
lumière encore intacte de la lune et il ne
se soucie pas plus de la vitesse de cette
lumière que de la rapidité ou de la lenteur
d'une chanson. Il écoute l'astre.
« Halo, ici Plaine-Lune, donnez-moi la
Terre urbaine. »
Sur la toile, Elsa répond.
(And if she paints an Indian it's the same
thing. He's astride his horse before the
cordillera in the still whole light of the
moon and he cares no more about the
speed of the light than about the rapidity
or slowness of a song. He's listening to
the star.
"Halo, Plain-Moon here, give me an
Earth line."
Upon the canvas, Elsa picks up the
phone.)

LÉGER

In March 1933, thirteen years before the publication of the
phenomenally successful *Paroles*, Fernand Léger, after witnessing a
performance of Prévert's *La Bataille de Fontenay (The Battle of
Fontenay*, 1,300-315) put on by the *Octobre* group, wrote to Léon
Moussinac: "Saw last week the *Octobre* group. Production by
Prévert. *Terrific play* and company. How is it that we haven't been
able to work with those people?"(AP, 91) In effect, Léger and
Prévert never would collaborate, despite continued mutual
admiration, until the death of the great Cubist artist in 1955, when the
journal *Aujourd'hui* planned a homage to Léger which led to Prévert
writing "Le Monde en vaut la peine" ("The World is Worth It",
2,534-7), a text accompanied by Gilles Ehrmann's photographs. The
title of Prévert's tribute to Léger, either a real or imaginary statement
attributed to Léger, immediately centers upon a fundamental tenet
pervading the poet's conception of creative activity: the latter is
dynamic, upbeat, joyous, and it is so because the world – within and
without – is a place of marvellousness, deep value and meaning. The

Cubist gesture, like all artistic gestures, may be, as poets such as Pierre Reverdy and Guillaume Apollinaire stressed along with Prévert, a gesture of transmutation of the given world, but it remains a celebration both of the simple (or even painful) things of the world and of the capacity within for such celebration and transformation. And, as Reverdy has argued, the world may exist "for art" – a seemingly post-Symbolist and post-Mallarméan position often associated with Cubism's aesthetic "interiority", but, equally, art is "for the world", "for life": its transmutations reinsert themselves in the world, enriching it, permitting us to better celebrate and appreciate its infinite potential for us, within us.

Prévert's text, symbiotically connected via its every unexpected twist and turn to Ehrmann's photos of Léger's studio and certain works, is personal in tone, full of evocations of specific elements of the artist's oeuvre, including his 1924 silent film *Le Ballet mécanique (The Mechanical Ballet)* made with the American Dudley Murphy. (Charles Poron argues less the Dadaist orientation of the yet non-linear anti-narrative of this film than its Cubist delight in what he terms "a dance of objects and fun fair accessories sketching out a simplified world" – one thus bound to please Prévert, of course.) In résumé, Prévert emphasises the following in his eulogy: 1. art *is* useful and its utility stems precisely from the beauty of the at once material, sensual and mental or emotional energies it releases; 2. Léger is a painter, every day, of the everyday, that is to say anything and everything, for all in life is valid, worthy, precisely because it *is* life – and this "despite" the apparent thematics of mechanisation and robotisation: such a thematics may be cautionary, but it entails great transmutation of a strictly aesthetic, imaginative, joyously creative nature; 3. Léger's entire vision, of life and art, is shrouded in "a great solid smile": this is a typical allusion both to the upbeat statement attributed to Léger which the title takes up, and to the peculiar podgy, cylindrical or solidly, clearly formed figures characteristic of much of Léger's work – and even his striking, ever-present signature; 4. *things* of the earth, recognisable and metamorphosed simultaneously in Léger's creations, are, as Prévert's imagined posthumous conversation between "a glass, a bottle, a chair, a hat on a hatstand" in Léger's house reveals – things "are a celebration and the celebration goes on, ephemeral but stubborn, that's about it and it's already a lot"; 5. Léger may "be" dead, but,

Prévert delights in wittily affirming, he "is", still: as Reverdy said in a famous essay on Braque, these paintings "are Braque",[1] that's essentially where the artist "is" – dead or alive; 6. life and art are fundamentally inseparable: despite our insistence upon difference, Prévert's experience of the world as he evocatively recounts flying over Paris in a helicopter is that "everything had the colors of Léger"; 7. in a pseudo-summary of what Léger's work "represents", Prévert cuts through typical modern intellectualisations and argues that the Cubist's work, no matter what its subject matter might be, remains "lovely to the eye, ... alive, calm, quick, useful and pleasing, ... sun, music, song"– no wonder Gilles Ehrmann, in recounting his coming to photography in *Jacques Prévert et ses amis photographes,* writes that the poet's views on his work were determining, for, rare phenomenon amongst critics, "he brought to [it] a poetic aura" (cf. 2,1288).

BRAQUE

Varengeville is the title of Prévert's short 1968 book presenting Georges Braque and in particular his seascapes executed in the small seaside town of that name, where, in effect, Braque is also buried. As Danièle Gasiglia-Laster emphasises (2,1318), Prévert's text brings out an element that especially delights this poet of the people, namely the nowadays easily overlooked pertinence of high quality art reproduction and dissemination via modern technology: art thus becomes available to the proletariat, cutting through class, snobbery, effete aestheticising and, perhaps, a proprietary intellectualisation of art – whereas all that matters, for Prévert, is the intensity of *pleasure* exchanged between artist and viewer (even by postcard reproduction): it is in this principle and practice of pleasure that art's meaning only can be *lived, felt.* Just like Reverdy who argues it of Braque and other artists such as Picasso, Léger, Matisse and Gris, Prévert emphasises the non-imitative character of Braque's work: what is at stake is "interpretation", what Gasiglia-Laster regards as the metamorphosed equivalency art provides, this perception, she rightly suggests, giving rise in turn to a corresponding highly metaphorised and at times nicely provocative anthropomorphic

---

[1] See *Note éternelle du présent,* loc. cit.

description by Prévert of what he sees in Braque's seascapes where sea and sky and land freely fuse their wonders: "The earth is my missus / the sea my woman of joy fear and anguish / says a seafaring song / But why do you imagine I should give a damn if she cheats on me with the wind / Even when she's awful she's so beautiful under the same sky".

Once again, in effect, Prévert quickly piles up aesthetic point upon aesthetic point, yet in the deftest of manners. Braque's seascapes, to him, speak implacably of the real, "dark salt-laden earth", "sun-drenched beaches", old "carcasses" of boats and plows. There is no fleeing from the world into fabricated exoticism or cerebral abstraction. Every phenomenon constitutes a microcosm that stands for the macrocosm. "Everything is in everything", Prévert writes. And the beauty of such metonymic exchange is that any choice Braque makes is capable of yielding the same marvelousness, the same pleasure, in exquisite miniature. Braque's work, Prévert points out, is not ludic in that it offers no gratuitous play of form; but, of course, as an "interpreter", a translator, he is a "solemn" and "intense" revealer of being. Interestingly, Prévert depicts Braque "gazing long at the color of waves / that color of nothingness", and he is thus close to poets such as Jacques Dupin and Bernard Noël who, whilst appreciating within both artistic and linguistic creation the pertinence of that strange metonymic equation Prévert observes between whole and fragment, also sense the equally strange "nothingness" – "no-time" and "no-space" Noël and Dupin both call it – at the heart of lived phenomena *and* artistically created form. Perhaps this is why Prévert can speak of Braque's "visual song", for createdness lies at the intersection of a fullness and yet that beautiful absence of content music so intangibly has us experience. To gaze upon Braque's seascapes is thus, for the spectator, as for the creator, to sense and feel "secrets exchanged / beauty divulged" – and this, as Prévert *so pertinently* remarks, beyond all rationalisable meaning: the meaning available involves, as with children, Prévert typically suggests, a saying / painting / observation / feeling without *knowing* exactly what one is in the process of intimately experiencing. Once more, Prévert sees art as a place / non-place of transfer of "marvel", "mirage" and beauty-in-metamorphosis, the whole transfer being enveloped in pleasure. Prévert's parting gambit is characteristic:

> [La mer] ne lui demande pas ce qu'est la peinture
> il ne lui demande pas ce qu'est la beauté
> dans les tarots de la peinture Braque est un seigneur
>> qui sait que son véritable pouvoir c'est de ne
>> pouvoir faire autrement que beau et vivant
> [The sea] doesn't ask him what painting is
> he doesn't ask it what beauty is
> in the tarots of painting Braque is a lord who knows
>> that his authentic power is not to be able to
>> make anything that isn't beautiful and alive)

Such knowing may frustrate those who wish to subtly rationalise and codify artistic activity, but it is largely sufficient for the artist who relies on the intensity of energy welling up within rather than its theorisation.

KLEE

One of the finest of Prévert's poems on art appeared in 1946 in *Cahiers d'art*, accompanied by two pieces from the 1920's by Paul Klee (who had died six years earlier). It is Prévert's only text devoted to Klee but it exemplifies the powerfully revealing uncomplicated exchange that can come about via free imaginative creation between spectator and artist. Here is Prévert's delightfully simple yet penetrating and felt untitled text, taken up again in the 1951 *Spectacle* (1,361-2), a poem more than rivalling in charm and insight his famous "Pour faire le portrait d'un oiseau":

> Parfois le balayeur
> poursuivant désespérément
> son abominable labeur
> parmi les poussiéreuses ruines
> d'une crapuleuse exposition coloniale
> s'arrête émerveillé
> devant d'extraordinaires statues
> de feuillages et de fleurs
> qui représentent à s'y méprendre
> des rêves
> des crimes des fêtes des lueurs
> des femmes nues une rivière l'aurore et le bonheur
> et le rire et puis le désir
> des oiseaux et des arbres
> ou bien la lune l'amour le soleil et la mort

Etranges monuments de l'instant même
élevés à la moindre des choses
par des indigènes heureux
et malheureux
et laissés là
généreusement offerts au hasard et au vent
ces statues se dressent
devant le balayeur qui n'en croit pas ses yeux
et qui met la main sur son coeur
en se sentant soudain
inexplicablement heureux
Et les statues balancent doucement
dans l'oseille du soleil couchant
leurs jolis corps de filles noires
drapés de pavots rouges et blancs
Et la statue du vent
toute nue derrière les statues d'arbres
fait retentir le bienveillant vacarme
de l'espace et du temps
Et la statue enfant terrifie le gendarme
par la seule grâce de son chant
et la lune bat la campagne
avec son grand fléau d'argent
Et le balayeur sourit
bercé et caressé
par la statue qui représente la fraîcheur de la vie
Et moi quand je regarde les tableaux de Paul Klee
je suis comme ce balayeur
reconnaissant
émerveillé
ravi
(Sometimes the sweeper
desperately laboring on with
his abominable sweeping
amongst the dusty ruins
of some sordid colonial exhibition
stops in wonder
before extraordinary statues
of leaves and flowers
with their life-like representation
of dreams
crimes fairs glimmerings
naked women a river dawn and happiness

and laughter and then desire
of birds and trees
of else the moon love the sun and death
Strange monuments of the now moment
raised up to the slightest of things
by happy and unhappy
natives
and left there
generously offered to chance and wind
statues rising up
before the sweeper who can't believe his eyes
and puts his hand on his heart
suddenly feeling
inexplicably happy
And the statues gently sway to and fro
in the sorrel of the setting sun
their pretty black girlish bodies
draped with red and white poppies
And the statue of the wind
naked behind the tree statues
echoes the benign din
of time and space
And the child statue terrifies the police officer
with the very grace of her song
and the moon scours the countryside
With her grand silvery scourge
And the sweeper smiles
lulled and caressed
by the statue representing freshness of life
And I when looking at Paul Klee's paintings
am like this sweeper
grateful
filled with a sense of marvel
entranced.)

The capacity of art to delight, enrapture and transfigure all of us emotionally, spiritually, is thus Prévert's central understanding gleaned from looking at Klee's work. Prévert's desire to see himself in the shoes of this night-sweeper reflects undoubtedly an instinctive anti-intellectual position in his discussion of art, but it emphasises to what extent he believes art, and all else in life, to be best understood through feeling, impulse, natural (though sympathetic) reaction. Certainly, Prévert's poem takes a dig at then still rampant colonialism. (The allusion to "happy and unhappy/natives" clearly evokes both Klee's admiration for "primitive" African art discovered by great European artists of the early part of the century, and the wretchedness often wrought upon their civilisation by colonial domination.) Art's celebration of *all and everything* is the otherwise significant insight the poem provides. And this celebration of all occurs beyond crass morality: a true unconditional celebration of life, *with* all its contradictions and contrasts, is what Prévert sees in Klee. And this, in turn, speaks of the innocence of all that is (including all we are). The very "strangeness" Prévert speaks of and sees in Klee, is the sign of life's endless differences, and it is precisely this difference or strangeness that provokes in the cleaner/Prévert joy, stimulation, discovery. A joy beyond reason, explanation, for none is needed. Klee's art caresses, comforts, reassures, reminds us all is well. And we are "grateful" for this, for the feeling that the *other* – all of life – is astonishing, strangely uplifting.

RIBEMONT-DESSAIGNES

It was, Prévert tells us, the painter-cum-writer Georges Ribemont-Dessaignes who was most instrumental in launching the poetry career of the author of *Paroles*. Saint-John Perse, too, played a critical early role in the first publication of "Tentative de description d'un dîner de têtes à Paris-France", but it was Ribemont-Dessaignes who invited Prévert to submit a text, first to *Bifur*, then to *Commerce*. Ribemont-Dessaignes, who had collaborated with Marcel Duchamp and Francis Picabia in pre-Dada work and who, like Prévert himself (fourteen years Ribemont-Dessaignes' junior), rejected Breton's Surrealist party-line, left Paris in 1934 for the inconspicuousness of small town life in the South (Villar-d'Arène – he had been born in Montpellier) and a relative solitariness that restored his life-long fascination with and desire for contact with nature's simplicities and beauties.

Two main texts devoted to Ribemont-Dessaignes' art will concern us here: "Itinéraire de Ribemont" ("Ribemont's Itinerary", 1,679-80) and *Arbres* (2,131-59).

The first of these was written for a 1951 exhibition of the artist's drawings held in Vence. The text was taken up in 1955 for the volume *La Pluie et le beau temps*. Ribemont-Dessaignes' work is seen by Prévert as "speaking landscape", an oeuvre generating great intimacy of exchange with flowers, roof tiles, sky, trees, paths and garden walls, the "sounds" and "silences" of either natural phenomena or phenomena in simple harmony therewith. "Landscape landscape / that's how I see you", writes a Prévert clearly in tune with the Bonnefoy of "Dedham, vu de Langham" ("Dedham, seen from Langham"), in which the praises of Constable are sung.[1] If Ribemont-Dessaignes would always feel the "hospitality" of the natural world, so, too, Prévert argues – with a philosopher such as Heidegger, or poets such as Guillevic or younger generation poets like Jean-Claude Pinson or Yves Leclair – does the natural world find "hospitality" in the art of Ribemont: a being at home, a "place of habitation", where ease of being and doing may prevail. Such an ease involves a "forgetting" of much else, "of a throng of things", and no doubt this is a reference to all that the recently ended war epitomises. But it is also a reminder that a painting is, as Prévert stresses when writing about Braque, a microcosmic, metonymic representation of a whole (: the entire world, the cosmos), a forgetting that is a specific concentration of attention emblematic of a greater, all-embracing gesture and "hospitality". A final, typically ludic flourish is provided by Prévert in his presentation of the paradox of, on the one hand, a process of painterly "captivation" and "capturing" and, on the other, the freedom resulting from this process – both for artists and "subject". The seemingly quirky concluding references to "the ostrich with its eyes shut", "the Emperor of China" and the "non-talking canary" complete this poem of profound appreciation of a fine friend, a powerfully discreet artist and an equally quirky writer: the references are all to Ribemont-Dessaignes' novelistic and theatrical writings of the 1921-24 period.

Arbres, of which I have already spoken in the context of Prévert's vast thematics of Earth, I should like to look at again briefly according to the optic that preoccupies us here. Appearing in book form in 1967 with Ribemont-Dessaignes' drawings which largely inspired the volume's ample range of texts, the latter go back, in effect, to 1955 (when Prévert wrote certain parts to accompany another Ribemont exhibition) and the early 1960's (when other pieces or amplifications could be read in review or in the 1963 *Histoires et*

---

[1] See *Ce qui fut sans lumière,* Mercure de France, 1987.

autres histoires). *Arbres* thus offers a mosaic of diversely conceived and styled texts. Irony, satire, sheer fun and emotional fervor intersect and conjoin to give a now political, now ethico-ecological, now more relaxedly "spiritual" flavor to this longish poem. The theme of a return to some "green paradise of love", as Danièle Gasiglia-Laster terms it (2,1047), is not just Baudelairian or Zolian, but could just as easily be thought Rousseauist or Hugolian or Lamartinian – *Jocelyn*, for example – as well as highly contemporary; and the refounding of our being, in Eve-Adamic "postmode", as it were, is not uncharacteristic of certain contemporary feminist poetics – one thinks of Hyvrard and, at times, Chawaf. Prévert liked to sign his dedications to friends "Jacques Rêve Vert" (Green Dream Jacques). As for Ribemont-Dessaignes, Prévert sees him here 1. as a "hunter of happiness", a non-violent hunter, of course, just as in the earlier text for the artist Prévert sees him as a liberating captor; 2. as on the side of life, far from the destructive speed of "men / [who] went so quickly nowhere / that they were all the time / anywhere / with great weird metal heaps / that everywhere spoilt everything"; 3. as conveying a sense of cosmic mystery – of the earth and beyond: "other stars / other trees / other beings perhaps"; 4. as someone capable – as we have seen Prévert often emphasise – of appreciation and "interpretation" without any need for justification or explanation: what so often fouls up humans, Prévert declares in a memorable passage, is its clinging to ideas – with their conditional rationalisations, "wars of ideas / fixed opinions and idea-harems" – whereas, he feels, the artist's only needed criteria are unconditional instinctive love of things, a natural desire to caress the latter's mystery and beauty; 5. as a consequent purveyor of a "madness" that is "wisdom", an equation matching Prévert's opening gambit picturing trees as "wild and wise horses / green-maned / ... / rearing up in the wind"; 6. as like those rare people who still carve their names in love on the sturdy bark of trees (and who are the only ones to be "spared" by the trees themselves in Prévert's closing scenario of the trees' uprising and self-liberation) – just as Prévert and Ribemont-Dessaignes may together be likened to trees carrying on – is there a poet elsewhere to have boldly delighted in such metaphor?! – the "first great soap opera" of the world.

CHARBONNIER

The work of Pierre Charbonnier, since first being exhibited in 1922 at the Théâtre de l'Oeuvre thanks to Lugné-Poe's kindness, has attracted much admiration from writers and especially poets. Jules Supervielle was the first to buy his work; Symbolists, Dadaists and Surrealists found varying strictly non-imitative echoes of their own preoccupations; René Char prefaced two post-war catalogues and collaborated in other creative ways with Charbonnier; Francis Ponge similarly wrote of his painting and was illustrated in turn by an artist he described as operating somewhere "between the best of Chirico and Seurat". Prévert himself knew Charbonnier in various contexts: his early films from the 1928-36 period; his vast pieces used by Diaghilev as decors in his ballet *Odes*; his various collaborations leading to the texts that interest us here, both from the 1950's.

The first of these texts, "Paysage" ("Landscape", 2,503-4), serving initially as an accompaniment to an invitation to an important 1956 Paris exhibition of Charbonnier's work, centers upon the tensional and productive relationship of control and freedom in the artist's aesthetics – a relationship that a poet such as Reverdy deemed central to all artistic gesture, and one that helps us understand why Charbonnier's work appealed to Symbolists and Cubists on the one hand (with their sense of proportion, harmony, order, equilibrium) and Dadaists and Surrealists on the other (tending to privilege automaticity, liberated expression, spontaneity, even utter phantasmagoria). Prévert, of course, always shying away – boldly, laughingly – from isms and prescriptive modes understands immediately that tensionality allowing creation to occur on a continuum linking, rather than separating, control and freedom. He understands, too, that the artist – Charbonnier here – always operates an *osmosis* between world and painting: again, the idea that art is remote from the world via its disorderings and reorderings seems ludicrous to Prévert: hence his charming and witty idea that Charbonnier "open[s] his window / upon real appearances": what we see is always appearance, but it is as real as art itself! Prévert thus cuts quickly through heavy-handed intellectualisations to stress the artist's sensitivity – in his work – to the sunlight on things, any and all things, that in turn can find their (transformed) place of revelation upon the "canvases of Charbonnier / ardent and calm landscapes" –

places of passion and desire, new energy and *joie de vivre*, as Prévert
writes, places too of "dreams stolen from children"; yet places of that
"calmness" that, as Reverdy argued, always inhabits the forms of
what is painted, no matter how transmuted or, as Rimbaud might
have said, unruly and disarranged.

The second of Prévert's typically compact, dense yet
delightfully, drolly transparent texts, "La Couleur de la lumière..."
(2,531-3) was first published, along with texts and documents by
Char, Ponge, Christian Zervos, Robert Bresson and others, in a small
book coming out to coincide with another important Paris exhibition
of Charbonnier's work. Always perspicacious, light-hearted, playful,
Prévert's text betrays profound admiration for an artist gazing out
upon the world and somehow capturing it "with tenderness distress
and friendship / with ardent lucidity". No verbiage, but simply
Prévert's recognition of the vital, emotional, meditative "clarity"– the
word is Prévert's – an artist like Charbonnier brings to bear on the
world around him, via his art: his interaction with and transformation
of the world. Again, art – like the world – can be exquisite in its
"oddly simple" fusion or non-differentiation of the real and the
apparent: all is both, simultaneously, whether a river or a painting
thereof. Prévert thus brings us face to face with the simple enigma,
the transparent mystery of life and art: both are "there", but what
they "are" is uncertain – but, then again, happily, it doesn't matter:
emotion, passion and love before both world and art are all that
matters to Prévert, and Charbonnier.

FROM CHAGALL AND GIACOMETTI TO VASARELY AND MAGRITTE

Prévert wrote about and for very many artists. Those treated
above may be said to have some place of honor, but Prévert never
plays favorites. No hierarchy is ever hinted at. Many lesser known
painters – Lucien Jacques, Fabra, Maïk, Pougny, Émilienne
Delacroix, Duhème, Labarthe, Papart, Odet and so on – draw his
enthusiastic attention which always centers on energy, desire,
simplicity, the "dance" (cf. 1,390) of natural, ever unique creativity.
Before taking a concluding look at Prévert's own artistic powers, I
should like to confirm much of the preceding analyses by skipping

through four more texts strongly emblematic of so much Prévert offered over the years to so many artists of his time.

In 1950 Prévert thus writes a wonderful presentation of the work Chagall produced "from" 15th century miniatures illustrating Boccaccio's *Decameron*: "Dans ce temps-là..." ("In Those Days...", 1,362-8). What strikes Prévert is the privileging of desire, desire working through contrast and contradiction, and a certain sensitivity to human ingenuity and "magicalness". The timeless dovetailing of the mediaeval imagination and that of Chagall turns about love, in the eyes of Prévert. Love unifies their gestures, places their images in the same "magic lantern" – a place of functioning, moreover, remote from modern aesthetic theory, not giving a fig for its not infrequent preciousness.

1966 sees Prévert offer to *Paris-Match* a short but powerful prose text – the Chagall text is in free verse – upon the death of Giacometti, whom Prévert had known from the 1920's. He evokes the artist's endless dissatisfaction – again the theme of desire –, his constant fluctuation between laughter and an "anger" that had nothing of an "artistic despair" Prévert tells us Giacometti found "uninteresting" (cf. "J'ai connu Giacometti..." ("I knew Giacometti ...", 2,579-80). But what Prévert deems centrally pertinent is Giacometti's "pursuit" of goals never really attainable: a determined commitment to the process of art, its "work", working through what one is doing – a working through, and on, which itself becomes the purpose of it all, via some strange tautology. Such a pursuit "obeys a need both for pleasure and something else" – Prévert's modesty and unpresumptuousness prevent him from specifying what this presumably meta-physical something might be, but he does recognise it and points to its unnameableness. Prévert is struck, too, as with other artists, that, no matter what the subject of Giacometti's work, what results is a "self-portrait". Alain Robbe-Grillet has recently turned the tables on New Novel and New Wave Film criticism by emphasising such an equation of self and other, subject and object. Therein, for Prévert, lies the "truth" of Giacometti, a traveller of his own mind, yet one strangely capable of offering to children, as to aestheticians, the fascination of the unique "beings" / being his art generates.

"Imaginoires" ("Blackimaginaries", 2,490-93) is the text Prévert prepared for the catalogue of the 1946 Paris exhibition of

Vasarely's work centered particularly on a thematics – and a formatics, if I may express myself freely – of zebra stripings, chess boards and harlequins where black and white magically combine to create new, illusionist, quasi-surreal forms, orders, with the equally new aesthetic emotion – "that emotion called poetry", Reverdy would call it – that necessarily accompanies them. Prévert speaks of Vasarely's "roundabout of images, faces and mirages / of life", thereby stressing that what is created and (black-)magically imagined *is* life: Vasarely's *are* the forms of life, new forms seen for the first time, not art-forms separate from life, but vestiges of life's energy surging forth in Vasarely's particular manner, here, now. Prévert thus stresses that this exhibition reveals to us not art as opposed to life, but art as a shifting, vibrant exploration of life's creative energy, resulting in new life forms.

The text Prévert devotes to the much admired Belgian painter Magritte is written for the catalogue of a major 1961 exhibition in London. It appears alongside many other homages, those, for example, of Breton and Eluard, as well as those of artists such as Lam, Ernst, Ubac and Arp. Prévert focusses his piece on the fused flagrancy and mystery of Magritte's "things and beings, and this and that". His originality stems from his mental availability, but it seeks not to explain or justify itself, nor to ostentatiously "impose itself". Its self-evidence, Prévert feels, has much greater simplicity about it – a favorite characteristic, as we have seen, of all the artists Prévert admires. Magritte's is yet an oeuvre that thrives via an aesthetics – the term is mine, as you will understand: Prévert wouldn't clog his pen with it unless to have fun at the user's expense – an aesthetics, *dis-je*, of rarity, beauty and surprise. It is this aesthetics, essentially, that allows "dream" and "truth" to marry with magical ease, and which allows Magritte's work always to be "there and elsewhere at the same time". Inimitable, delightful, insightful criticism, indeed...

PRÉVERT'S COLLAGES

In 1943 Prévert makes for his wife Janine the beautiful collage we see almost at the end of *Fatras* with her photograph framed by leaves and flowers, nuts and cones. It is a gift they will treasure and that will adorn Prévert's study entrance all his life. A few years later in 1948, during his long convalescence after the fall from the window of the Paris Radiodiffusion studio, Prévert patiently cuts out endless pieces from his already huge collection of images, pasting together fragments of engravings, photographs, postcards, magazine pictures, lithographs and so on. For the next twenty-nine years he will continue with passion and concentration this practice of the collage. In 1963 an exhibition of his work is presented in Antibes: some one hundred and twelve pieces already; and in Paris in December of the same year Picasso "dedicates" the catalogue to a similar exhibition. 1966 sees the publication of *Fatras* with its fifty-seven reproductions of many of Prévert's best collages. In 1970, *Imaginàires* appears in the *Sentiers de la Création* series with Skira, and once more Prévert's collages are offered significant limelight, intertwined as they are once more with written texts of varying tonality and mode. Five years after Prévert's death, Gallimard publishes *Jacques Prévert, Collages*, with a preface by Philippe Soupault, a substantial text by André Pozner and a very considerable selection of the almost two hundred collages of Prévert that are known to exist.

Max Ernst, whom Prévert regarded as a master fabricator of the collage, saw the latter, in characteristically Surrealist perspective, as the product of a "fortuitous encounter" of disparate elements. As Pozner rightly points out, however – we go back in some respect here to the Reverdy-Breton debate over the degree of conscious intervention of the mind in the creation of the image[1] – Prévert's tactics involve premeditation, a conjoining not of pure chance-driven elements, a conjoining that is purposeful, involving both a retention of the "real" and its derailment, its staged transgression, its fabrication of a cinema whose narrative provokes, opens debate and still constitutes a "puzzle", as Prévert calls it – for the collage remains a fragmented (non-)structure, never offering that "full picture [that] is one of the elements of contemporary deception and foolishness" (JPC, 9). If, then, the phantasmagorical jubilancy of Prévert's collages, with their juxtapositional or fusional psychic energy, is matched by an orchestrated non-gratuitousness, the meanings emanating from this conscious if spontaneous purposing of fabrication never, in Prévert's

---

[1] See "Trente-deux lettres inédites à André Breton", *Etudes littéraires*, Apr. 1970; and M. Bishop, "Pierre Reverdy's Conception of the Image", *Forum for Modern Language Studies,* Jan. 1976.

mind, can be said to claim for themselves a stability, an ideology, a "totality" – or totalitarianism – he, in effect, abhors.

This it is important to bear in mind in looking at Prévert's collage work. *Fatras* is the title of the volume in which such work is first represented. Danièle Gasiglia-Laster has shown very well the range of connotation the word *fatras* deploys and the light thus cast not only upon Prévert's written texts but also upon his collages (cf. 2,957-62); and René Bertelé sees these Prévertian collages as subversion, rather than pure reconstruction or reassembly, of meaning. In this sense, Prévert's plastic art is not unlike that underpinning his poetry, though the collages of *Fatras* clearly make no effort of mimetism in relation to the volume's poems. "Prolongations", Gasiglia-Laster terms them (2,959), another means of multiplying those extremely plural and expanding, elastic types of (self-)articulation that are at the heart of Prévert's originality. In the 1982 Gallimard volume Pozner offers the beginnings of a primitive typology of the representations Prévert's collages offer: "about twenty angels, about sixty animals some of which are the Good Lord's, fifteen Christs, four clowns, ten Sacred-Hearts, eighteen beheadings, eleven God-the-Fathers, one Teilhard de Chardin, one *voyeur*, two owl-headed men, three bat-headed men, six painters, about twenty saints, three Napoleons, one dwarf-sized, etc., etc." (JPC, 13). *Fatras* certainly reveals such elements and many others at times difficult to categorise or even describe: strange objects and scenes, women and children embroiled in the latter, groupings of creatures and phenomena in interaction or seeming suspension or dissociation despite proximity, creatures elaborately dressed or offered naked, vulnerable yet powerfully present, exquisite or utterly reduced, or, yet again, caught in ambiguous semi-dressed states. Flagrancy dominates – this is the realness, the thereness of Prévert's representations –, but so too does enigmaticalness, ambivalence, uncertainty. Menace lurks so often implicitly in the *contra*-dictions that Prévert deploys: the "discourses" of innocence, beauty, love, ease vying with those of violence, constraint, domination or mere indifference, for example. This does not mean that fun and exhilaration are absent – the child leaping over the grotesque figure of Death (in *L'Échappée belle* (*A Close Call*, 2,32)), the portraits of Picasso, Miró and Janine, or the four *Souvenirs de Paris* (*Paris Souvenirs*, 2,113-14) all convey in varying ways the joyful buoyancy of both the imagination and life as it can be lived beyond fear, perversion, distortion. But globally speaking the collages of *Fatras* articulate a high tensionality, cultural perhaps more than ontological, yet running deep and vitiating the natural verve of being that could be ours – and that the provocation and stimulation of the collage restores to us, if we will.

Imaginaires (2,162-97) continues Prévert's extraordinary picture show, offering us, in the place of the endless images of our modernity that flatly reproduce, a series of images driven by dream and imagination, by a teeming infinite real yet threatened by mass production, warfare, power, economic hegemony, cultural cleansing. The flatness of our (self-)representation is thus provoked, given depth, deconstruction and reconstruction simultaneously. It is the real presented consciously yet "higgledy piggledy, a really beautiful language", as Prévert, witty and witting to the last, puts it. The collage thus adopts the language of defiant, dis-believing dis-order. As Gasiglia-Laster rightly points out, moreover, children and especially women are so often at the center of such purposing invitations to re-order, to metamorphose our reigning social and psych(olog)ical structures. Woman, here, may be seen as a refused, resisted yet desired locus of beauty, suppleness, mystery, independence, innocence and mischievous unpredictability. Her image runs counter to the banal, constraining norms of masculine rationalisms. Her dis-ordering, like Prévert's, disturbs and challenges, completely natural and simply life-affirming though it may be – no doubt *because* it is. Her presence and "meaning", like Prévert's via his collages, are synonymous with recreation and re-creation, joy in, and transformation of consciousness of, our very being. Imaginaries, indeed. A glance at the opening collage of the volume with its long handwritten title-cum-inscription (: *No image is immediate, all are in the far, the soon, the near or the late*, 2,162) and its bizarre, mind-bending amalgam of human and half-human, animal and mutated forms, everything set in a space at once intimate, familiar, and rationally unstabilisable, defiant – such a glance reveals an artist beyond congealed truths, caught up himself in the continuous swirl of his interrogations of the real and the *contra*-dictions the latter uncover and display. Other collages, it is true, are less puzzling and, whilst dealing with the world's many opposing discourses or emblems (natural beauty, sexuality, desire vs. control, fear, criminalisation as in *Salutiste contestant l'érotisme (Salvation Army Member Contesting Eroticism*, 2,186); or the pleasure and conceivable tribulation of smoking as in the delightfully titled *Monument élevé à la très douce sorcière Nicotine (Monument in Honor of the Most Sweet Sorceress Nicotine*, 2,194), clearer, though whimsical, paradoxical and not just contestatary, in the interfolded messages they convey. However, many retain an aura of profound strangeness and enigmaticalness that ally *Imaginaires* with the Surrealists and their fascination with the Marvelous, with Breton's Convulsive Beauty, with that point in the universe which Breton again saw as a locus of resolution of all apparent polarities and rationalised, moralised or aestheticised oppositions.

Philippe Soupault picks up on this latter point in his Preface to the 1982 volume *Jacques Prévert, Collages*, speaking of a "liberation [that] is further extended by each collage" (JPC, 6). "Jack in Wonderland", Soupault ends up calling his friend from the 1920's. Far from being a mere diversion, Prévert's collages are seen as integral to his vocation as a questioner of the world's ways and modes of being, a liberator centered upon the "fantastic" and the "unimaginable" both as a place of existential problem and wondrous, naturally utopian transcendence of such problem. Wit, wonderment, jubilant interrogation and transmutation, sheer play and serious (un)imaginable re-creation, redefinition of our being – yes, all of these elements inform the shifting, magical picture show Prévert's collages perform. At the close of this final tribute to Prévert's collaging imagination, however, come a series of pieces grouped under the rubric "Monsters". And whilst Prévert himself did not categorise certain collages according to such a designation – nor did he propose the grouping as it is offered us – it remains true that, not only towards the end of his life (when he tells André Pozner, "that's all I can see, everywhere"), but throughout, the monstrous has a significant place in *l'imaginaire* of the author of *Paroles*. In large part, of course, the monster is a natural observable phenomenon, a figure of war, violence, repression, ideology, fanaticism, intellectual distortion, psychological or emotional abuse and so on. In this sense, one could argue a persistent hauntedness in Prévert of which the monstrous is the sign. On the other hand, the fantastic, which includes the monstrous, remains a zone of play, of jubilant counter-provocation in addition to the fact that certain "monster" collages (such as the untitled one, JPC, 237, showing a strange female face, de- or re-formed, insect-like, even plant-like in part) merge the grotesque with the beautiful and, seemingly, beyond any sociopolitical intention. Certainly, a darker side to Prévert's vision is represented in some of his "monsters" – though, again, this is not Prévert's own appellation. *But,* each collage of such orientation remains a created, fabricated response *equally.* In this way, each "monster" constitutes an act of domination and appropriation of the *very* forces that might have crushed the poet's spirit. In this perspective, all the "monster" collages retain a powerful resiliency: they are not fearful, traumatised, retreating, but ever on a (whimsical, even if obsessive) counter-attack. They remain signs for, of, life; they continue to flow the vital energy within; they represent a profoundly *other* means of reaffirming (Prévert's belief in) love and beauty, joy and exuberance.

> la simple magie des choses et des
> êtres
> (the simple magic of things and
> beings)
> Jacques Prévert ("Eternité
> instantanée"
> ("Instant Eternity", 2, 663))

There is nothing neatly circumscribed and ordered about the creative evolution of Jacques Prévert, the unfolding of his genius in the realms of film, theater, poetry, song, art and photography. No partitions rear up, none are allowed to impose themselves. Freedom of creativity and collaboration is the one constant in a swirling aesthetics of spontaneously interwoven imaginative endeavor. If, then, I have chosen – as with the assessment of Prévert's pictorial collaborations, appreciations and creations, and as with my discussion to come of the pertinence of song to an understanding of his oeuvre – to in some measure separate out film activities from theatrical involvements or photographic collaborations, it is helpful to bear in mind that Prévert so often is working simultaneously and chiasmally on projects modally distinct and that one project feeds frequently into another. Cinematographic scenarios, ballets, short plays, poems, songs, artwork of his own or of others, photography and text – all, whilst maintaining their identity, also fuse, mutate, interact and criss-cross, establishing a space of imaginative accomplishment happily escaping the grasp of over-eager reductive categorisation.

FILM: BEGINNINGS

In *Elle* magazine, in 1959, Prévert speaks both of his weekly childhood visits to the local Pantheon cinema and of the very old films one could watch at the Gobelins sipping a glass in the cinema café. Of the former, which showed new silent films, "light comedies" capable of provoking "inextinguishable laughter" and starring Gribouille, Nick Winter or Rigadin, or "anguishing dramas", Prévert writes:

Behind the screen there was a man who made all the noises with a little contraption that didn't look like much: bells, sandpaper, a whistle, a revolver, hammers; and that was the storm, the wind and the sea or birdsong. It all went on at the same time as the piano playing. On Sundays, when there was a Far West film, an actor dressed up as a cowboy narrated the film swinging his lasso. Once, during *Le Massacre (The Massacre)*, a terrifying film in which the Indians were killing all the soldiers pulled back behind their wagons, the music, the noise, the shooting were making such a racket that the displeased spectators were screaming they couldn't see anything anymore. (2,249)

Both in "Enfance" and in the 1967 homage to the pioneer cineast Louis Feuillade (2,660-61), Prévert lists some of the earliest films he saw and loved, long before his initial involvements as an extra, then as assistant director and, finally, script-fixer and writer of full scenarios: *Le Vautour de la Sierra (The Vulture of The Sierras)*, *Morgan le Pirate (Morgan the Pirate)*, Tom Mix's Westerns, Rio Jim films, an early *Spartacus*, and so on.

If this childhood fascination was to persist with simple yet magical images contrasting blacks and whites arguably emblematic of the sentimental tensions and oppositions of early, popular film, and if, with Yves Tanguy, in 1922, Prévert was to confirm his love for cut-and-pasted images taken from daily newspapers and weekly magazines, it was not until 1928-29 that his professional entry into the world of cinema really took place. As Prévert tells André Pozner in *Hebdromadaires*, this brought him, for the first time, a job offering real pleasure, self-expression and adequate means (2,839). Scorned by the cultural elite it might be, lacking all academic or theoretical foundation it certainly was, but this made cinema all the more appealing to Prévert. If it was a "fair-like", populist mode of entertainment (cf. 2,839), this instinctively spoke to Prévert's sense of the naturally poetic depth of all that is real, his sense of an urgent tense beauty within the very drama of the everyday and in no need of effete aesthetic embellishment.

FILM: PREFERENCES

The besieged but quickly self-liberating inhabitants of the Baladar Islands, as Prévert portrays them in his 1932 *Lettre des Iles*

Baladar, determine only to retain one item of the "civilisation" of the Great Continent: cinema – not, moreover, that cinema, so invasive, so propagandist, conveying news and events of fatuous banality (: "military march-pasts, documentaries about peacock hunting", 2,553), but a self-generated cinema of imagination and "heart", of mind and emotion. Prévert's preference for a film such as Nico Papatakis' 1963 *Les Abysses (The Abysses)* – inspired, like Genet's *Les Bonnes (The Maids)*, by the 1932 Papin sisters affair – stems from his sense of the film's deep and strange realism. The two women are "two sisters in reality. / They are as beautiful as night and day, as mad, cruel and tender as life so often is" (2,648). And he adds, to avoid all ambiguity – though the criterion of beauty remains almost mystical in its Hugolian and Baudelairian dimensions: "In this film, what strikes most is not its unbearable savagery, nor its insolent aggressiveness, its furtive humor or its hidden tenderness. It isn't, either, its camera work, its technique, its style of dazzling simplicity, but quite simply its beauty". No preference given to ideology, social program, aesthetic theory, professional skill and the like; Prévert not so much deconstructs such niceties as he merely sweeps them to one side. The film conveys something much more important – and amazingly so, given its subject-matter –, namely the intrinsic beauty of the experience of being alive, feeling, seeing, beyond the endless categories that can ensnare and limit such experience of the ecstatic within the bewildering.

Film, then, may indeed be an art form, contrary to many early overly "refined" attitudes to its "primitivism", but its purpose is not to dwell in the rarefied atmosphere of art. The film Prévert prefers, either to make or to watch, is always, as he says in his 1957 "Actualités" (a quasi-commentary on Billy Wilder's film about Charles Lindbergh), "the film of love, the film of life" (1,891). It will thus escape the intellectual or epicurean pretentiousness of artist or critic, just as it will flee all non-poetic perspectives on life or art. He prefers a "sparrow's-eye" view to that of what he wittily calls, in "Gens de plume" ("Quill People", 1,355-6), "la Nouvelle Oisellerie Française" ("The New French Bird Shop") – a smiling dig at the *Nouvelle Revue Française* crowd. No, for Prévert, a film such as Bunuel's *Los Olvidados*, whilst centered on a reality dear to Prévert – the severe abuse of young delinquent and highly unloved children –, cuts through both aesthetic effeteness and crass bourgeois politics to focus on the emotion of existence, the capacity for joy and "sunny smile" in the midst of artificiality, officialdom, everything we can think matters more than love and happiness (cf. 1,339-41). Louis Feuillade's "primitive" work, "marvellously new, popular, alive", as Prévert (thinking of the 1913-14 *Fantômas* series beloved of the Surrealists) writes alongside homages of Alain Resnais, Marcel Allain and Georges Franju, is admired not dissimilarly for its ability to see the extraordinary in the everyday, to project "the disturbing eloquence of dream [via] the esperanto of silence", the sheer poetry of existence surging forth mysteriously yet manifestly from the simplicity/complexity of the lives of so-called ordinary people.

FILM: CREATIONS

One might reasonably argue that Jacques Prévert's film career was truly launched only with his collaboration with Jean Renoir in the production of the 1935 *Le Crime de Monsieur Lange (The Crime of Mr. Lange)*. But, of course, as with all critical turning-points, a trail leads up to this significant creative moment. Following some small part acting in 1924, Prévert's next few years see developing friendship and daily exchange with many young writers and artists: Aragon, Desnos, Péret, Leiris, Crevel, Breton; Giacometti, Masson, Ernst, Ribemont-Dessaignes. His very good friend Marcel Duhamel determines to go into film-making and in 1928 with Pierre Prévert, produces *Souvenirs de Paris (Paris Memories)*, based on an idea of Jacques Prévert. 1928 sees Christiane Verger put to music one of Prévert's very first texts, *Les Animaux ont des ennuis (Animals have Problems)*, written for the dancer Georges Pomiès (who will later work with Isadora Duncan). More creative contacts ensue in the nascent film world, with Auriol, Tual, Batcheff and others, and Prévert works on various scenarios, acts in Bunuel's 1930 *L'Age d'or (The Golden Age)* and, in 1931, patches up scenario and script for *Baleydier*, starring Michel Simon. The next two years produce, moreover, two classics of their kind: the 1932 *L'Affaire est dans le sac*, a promisingly poetically eccentric film produced by Prévert's brother Pierre and one Prévert always maintained was his favorite creation; and the 1933 *Ciboulette*, involving Prévert's adaptation of De Flers' operetta in the direction of what Roger Boussinot terms a "poetic caricature".

Prévert's cinematographic experience was, then, by the time of adapting Renoir's scenario for *Le Crime de Monsieur Lange* and writing all its dialogue material, really quite extensive and varied. The film, starring Florelle, René Lefèvre, Jules Berry and Marcel Lévesque, explores not only the emotional and ethical tensions of criminality, judgement and innocence, but those that oppose and interweave laughter and trauma, gaiety and existential difficulty. As with so much of Prévert's work, moreover, the power of love remains of central pertinence in the lives of "ordinary" people, for he sees it as involving the deployment of the splendor of their psychic energy. Human capacity, its sheer "innocence" beyond our banal moralising categorisations, will always fascinate Prévert. The film may have a spatio-temporal specificity – Claire Blakeway argues its political thrust even[1] – but it equally conveys powers and energies not limited by such specificity, merely framed and revealed thereby. The *mise en abyme* technique offering a narration within narration is not chosen for its aesthetic cleverness, but because it too confirms that taut relationship of the real and the mysterious, beautiful forces at the heart of the real – beyond sociology and psychological rationalising, inaccessible to our often presumptuous philosophical overlaying.

A year later, in March of 1936, begins that rich period of intense creative collaboration between Prévert and the producer-director Marcel Carné. The film, *Jenny*, notable for its so-called "poetic realism" allows Prévert to meld the exquisite and the everyday, to fuse the touching and the marvellous with the rugged and the seemingly humdrum. Time and place thus again dig deeply within the emotional energy investing them to reveal "poetic" dimensions within the real that astonish and move. (Prévert's witty song, "Cosy Corner", written for the young actor Marcel Mouloudji to perform, was finally censored for silly political reasons.) The next few years prove to be wonderfully creative and Prévert's own contributions are happily matched by his rich and lasting appreciation of the genius of so many actors, artists, musicians and persons of imaginative enthusiasm with whom he shared this period of exhilarating and free expansion. When he thus thinks back to the 1937 *Drôle de drame (Funny Affair)*, the 1938 *Quai des brumes (Wharf of Mists)* or the 1939 *Le Jour se lève (Daybreak)*, Prévert so

---

[1] Claire Blakeway's study is perceptive throughout.

often emphasises the creative genius of Trauner's decors with their "imaginary architecture / of dreams and bits of plaster light and wind / ... so beautiful and so alive" (2,627-8). Or he might stress the significance of Maurice Jaubert's compositional work, with its magical mood shifts, a "music tender and happy, sad and gay, simple and beautiful; a music truly of the people" 2,628); or, yet again, the fine collaborations of actors such as Michel Simon or Jean Gabin, Simon who "has no label, [who] belongs to no school of admiration"(2,649); Gabin who is "evidence itself / the very proof of a human being / who plays out his role in public / before so many others who play out theirs in secret" (2,631).

If *Drôle de drame* – despite becoming what Georges Unglik calls "a classic of French burlesque" with, as Jean-Louis Barrault explains, its "total freedom of expression and its synthesis of humor and poetry" – received a coolish welcome, *Le Quai des brumes*, starring Gabin and Michèle Morgan, had an altogether warmer one. Prévert's dialogues, tight, richly tacit, perfectly conscious of all that hovers in the mind and heart between the words we utter, are in complete harmony with the tensions of the film's narrative, its understated but strongly felt emotional intensity. There are vague links with *Le Crime de Monsieur Lange* – it is at bottom a tale of murder and escape –, but above all the film theatricises and visually represents powerful human emotions and impulses: the pure beauty of love with no strings attached, essential gestures and modes of an ordinary hero and heroine somewhat illumined and transfigured by the instinctual deployment of their presence, their aliveness. If "good" and "evil" are perceptible here, Prévert never moralises, overtly politicizes or intellectualises them, just as the "tragic" is subsumed within a much vaster, unsentimentalised realm of lyricism. This makes for a sense of resiliency – which is not just that of courageous struggle – where, otherwise, melancholy could have drowned out the energy of the "heroic" *coup de foudre*. A certain timelessness prevails too, despite the film's earthy, anchored quality, and this is subtly fostered by the elegant economy of the dialogues and the film's rhythmic structuring.

The 1939 *Le Jour se lève* once again brings together Jean Gabin and the writer/producer team of Prévert and Carné. It also stars the two remarkable actresses Arletty and Jacqueline Laurent. Love and death once more tussle together as a crime of passion explodes in the midst of the lives of "ordinary" people – people, that is, who come to a spectacularly full sense of their own emotional and visceral intensity, specificity, uniqueness. Not a rationalised sense, of course, but a directly experienced sense of their desires, their fascinations, their complicatedness as well as their beautiful simplicity. What comes across both via Prévert's finely modulated dialogues that so subtly let in the endless unsaids of our shifting mental and affective states, and via Carné's haunting images so in harmony with Prévert's script, is precisely the deep poetry of human exchange and psychology. The fundamental innocence of the good perpetrator of the crime of passion thus blends with the compassion of ordinary people faced with the latter. It is perhaps true that neither Prévert nor Carné can let go of the temptation to polemicise their thematics of the incredible violence of those in authority – here, the police, but we are on the eve of a war Prévert despised from all sides – and a whole ethics lies at once implicit and flagrant in the thematics of the hunted, cornered man. Good and bad do thus fly their flags in this film that both pictures, and is part of, the world of popular entertainment – although the thematics of misunderstanding, obsession and the mystery of motivation may be argued to, at least implicitly, extend "recuperation" to all humans, all action, all ideology, no matter how much in contradiction with both the power of gentleness and love, and the complex, paradoxical "heroic" violence that may develop, impulsively, explosively, seemingly from the latter.

In the same year that *Le Jour se lève* comes out, Prévert is called up for military service only to be "invalided" in March 1940 for silly and provocative behavior. Some months later, having made his way south to Nice and the village of Tourrette-sur-Loup in the company of the Kosmas, Brassaï and his "estranged" wife Simone, Prévert resumes his cinematographic activities, working on a *Chat botté (Puss in Boots)*, *Une femme dans la nuit (A Woman in the Night)* which comes out late in 1941, and Pierre Billon's *Le Soleil a toujours raison (The Sun is Always Right)*, first shown – in the unoccupied South – in late November. From this time until the summer of 1942, Prévert, working with Pierre Laroche, concentrates principally on scenario and script for Carné's *Les Visiteurs du soir (Night Visitors)* which not only stars Arletty, Roger Blin and Jules Berry, but also the young Simone Signoret and Alain Resnais.

It is in 1943 that are born the initial idea and desire that will lead two years later to the final production and screening of one of the greatest classics of French cinema, *Les Enfants du paradis* (*The Children of Paradise*). Trauner's decors triumph, as does Kosma's music, and at the center unfold the masterly dialogues of Prévert in a scenario he again superbly imagines for the subtle producing hand of Marcel Carné. The cast is exceptional: Jean-Louis Barrault, Arletty, Pierre Brasseur, Maria Casares, Marcel Herrand, Jane Marken, Pierre Renoir, Fabien Loris, Jacques Castelot, Robert Dhéry, Paul Frankeur, Albert Rémy, Jean Carmet, Gérard Blain... If this is a truly great film, however, it is because it accomplishes a vast sweep through the lives of many, reveals the remarkableness of their dreams and actions, shows how life is an immense theater of self-creation and co-creation, situates each individual ever at the center of the swirling dance of being, manifests the endless contrasts on the equally endless gamut of emotion and response, consent and resistance in relation to our teeming desires. Prévert stages in this way, and half-articulates through all that his dialogues say and leave unsaid, the vast drama of all existences, separate and interwoven, puzzling in their contradictions and half-intuited in their so easily overlooked beauty and extraordinariness. Questions and flashing insights swarm and abound in the words and the crevices of human exchange. Judgement is declined; a strange quality hovers about despite the pockets of "criminality", and, perhaps above all, life is always perceived as potential *fête*, wondrous and beautiful celebration of what at best we can be, regardless of sadness or fear or self-doubt. Great emotional depths are thus plumbed with deftness and discretion, far from the grand emblems and language of our classical myths, in touch rather with the speech and gestures of all those who people the streets and cities of our modernity, faceless but magnificent, anonymous but passionately rising above the rote and routine that threatens to drown their spontaneity and their imagination, their joy and their love.

In this year and the next two or three, Jacques Prévert's cinematographic career could be said to peak, for the publication in 1946 of the astonishingly popular *Paroles* operates something of a shift of creative endeavor in Prévert. The year *Les Enfants du paradis* appears thus also sees the release of the cartoon *La Bergère et le ramoneur* (*The Shepherdess and the Chimney Sweep*), Prévert's adaptation from Andersen's tales in a collaboration with Paul

Grimault; at the beginning of 1946 the short poetic documentary *Aubervilliers,* produced by Eli Lotar, reaches the public with Prévert's songs and commentary on the wretched conditions prevailing in Aubervilliers at the time; at the close of the same year *Les Portes de la nuit (The Gates of Night)* is released with Yves Montand and Nathalie Nattier in the principal roles and Serge Reggiani, Jean Vilar, Dany Robin, Sylvia Bataille and Pierre Brasseur in the supporting cast. As usual in this Carné film – originally destined to star Marlene Dietrich with Gabin – Prévert's creative inventiveness is everywhere apparent: scenario, dialogues, two songs that soon will be world-famous, sung here by Fabien Lorris, or hummed by Montand and Nattier: *Les Enfants qui s'aiment (Children in Love)* and *Les Feuilles mortes (Autumn Leaves)*. 1947 sees Prévert and Carné combine imaginations once more, this time picking up a project abandoned in 1936 on children's gaols *(L'Ile des enfants perdus (The Island of Lost Children))*. Once more, however, the seemingly fated work – a fabulous cast had been assembled: Arletty, Martine Carol, Anouk Aimé and many others – stopped short of completion and even what was filmed was subsequently lost. In the spring of the same year, however, Prévert successfully joins forces with his brother Pierre to produce *Voyage-Surprise (Surprise Journey)*, in which Martine Carol does finally star, alongside Annette Poivre, Sophie Sel, Maurique Baquet and Lucien Raimbourg; and the next year, 1948, Prévert again adapts an Andersen tale to create, with Paul Grimault, the cartoon *Le Petit Soldat (The Little Soldier)*.

Two more films essentially bring to an end Prévert's very significant and often genial contribution to the world of film: the 1956 *Notre-Dame de Paris* by Jean Delannoy, starring Gina Lollobrigida and Anthony Quinn, and the 1961 *Les Amours célèbres (Famous Loves)*, a film by Michel Boisrond. *Notre-Dame de Paris* is finely adapted from Victor Hugo by a poet whose deep sense of the emotion of the "people" parallels that of France's greatest writer of the nineteenth century. Swarming street scenes fill the screen; the richly contrastive dimensions of popular masses is subtly played upon; satire, of church, state, science, the courts, melds with an intense exploration of love's "contradictions", revelations, repressions. Powerful, lyrically articulated tensions juxtapose deconstructive ambitions and remaining impulses to figure the ubiquitousness of beauty, innocence, heroism. Prévert's script offers a sweeping, lushly if contrivedly projected vision of passion and "madness", social constraint and the individual will for freedom and simple joy. Dance, music, song give expression to more deeply recessed psychic and physical pulsions. If much remains, in Hugo as in Prévert, subversive, such subversion always focusses ultimately on transformation, residual human splendor, an emotional, even moral knottedness ever set against the simplicity and innocence out of which grow even the worst of perversions and, of course, the more manifest nobleness of spirit that strives to transcend them. Boris Vian, let it be said in conclusion, makes a superbly vitiated Cardinal!

A few other creations round off the grandiose spectacle that is *Notre-Dame de Paris*: the 1964 telefilm *Le Petit Claus et le Grand Claus (The Big and the Little Santa)*, adapted from Hans Andersen; the 1966 *À la belle étoile (Under the Stars)*, again created with Prévert's brother, Pierre, and adapted from a short story by O'Henry; the 1969 *Le Chien mélomane (The Music-loving Dog)*, with Prévert's scenario for Paul Grimault's production. These final creations certainly demonstrate the full range of Prévert's imaginative impulse and, just as Mallarmé's *vers de circonstance* strangely blend with his *Coup de dés (A Throw of the Dice)*, so do these closing fantasies fuse seamlessly in so many ways with both the earlier work with Carné and the brilliantly and intensely colored tensions of the heart that *Notre-Dame de Paris* at once brashly and delicately portrays. Let it be said, too, that in 1974 Prévert goes back to the roots of his film work by recording and introducing texts of the *Octobre* group for a radio program of Gérard Descotils'; and in 1975 a show is mounted by the National Dramatic Center of Franche-Comté: Jacques Prévert and the *Octobre* group. Full Circle.

THEATER: *OCTOBRE*

In April 1932, shortly after the suicide of the actor Pierre Batcheff of whom Prévert had become a close friend, a number of breakaway members from the would-be revolutionary troupe *Prémices* approached Prévert for his help in creating a new repertory whose aims would not be simply self-serving aestheticism but rather social consciousness-raising and provocation. A month or so later the *Octobre* group – soon to become the most important of a good number of antifascist and left-wing pacifist groups, and rechristened after initially calling themselves simply the *Groupe de choc Prémices* – was performing Prévert's *Vive la presse (Long Live the Press)*, a creation of collaged newspaper cuttings offering polemical commentary on contemporary life and times. October of the same year confirms a collaboration that will last for some four full years: Prévert writes his celebrated *Bataille de Fontenoy (The Battle of Fontenoy)*, which *Octobre* will perform in January 1933 at the 2nd Congress of the French Workers' Theater Federation. Marcel Carné, then a journalist, describes it as follows: "It was a wild, baroque play, full of grating humor, vaguely Surrealist and anti-war into the bargain" (cf. 1,1157). Performed on various occasions over the next few years, and each time partially rewritten by Prévert typically to take account of contemporary events, *La Bataille de Fontenoy* – as the exemplary scholarship of Arnaud Laster and Danièle Gasiglia-Laster shows – presents six, at times significantly variant, versions. The original version was chosen, by referendum, to go to the 1933 Moscow Workers' Theater Olympics, where, not surprisingly, *Pravda* offers it a warm welcome: "The French group *Octobre* has put on a most interestingly staged review [whose] main interest [...] lies in the fact that the entire text is composed of press cuttings, bits of parliamentary speeches, aphorisms about political leaders. Many of the review's caricatures are masterfully done" (cf. 1,1159). Buoyed by such a reception, Prévert nevertheless refuses to sign a document backing Stalin's policies and actions of which, of course, little or nothing was known at the time in the West.

The 1933-1934 period sees Prévert write many agit-prop texts for *Octobre*. All are non-conformist, anti-establishment creations, at once ironic, farcical and yet socially and politically provocative. One may think at times of Jarry or Artaud, certain Surrealist and, of course, Dadaist texts, and then there is the popular tradition exemplified by Feydeau. Claire Blakeway has written very well on such dimensions. Yet Prévert's dramatic work, in collaboration with *Octobre*, whose ranks swell in successive waves during its brief existence, no doubt partly in response to the sheer verve of the material at its disposal – Prévert's dramatic work retains great specificity and is anything but mimetic: its texts tend to great brevity, almost joke-like compactness; they prefer darting allusion to overstatement; they are often not perceived as written-and-to-be-read texts, but rather flexible, performable bases highly dependent on imaginative and vigorous, passionate yet laughing interpretation. This is true, for example, of the throw-away pieces *Le Bel Enfant (The Lovely Child)* and *Un drame à la cour (Drama at Court)*; it is true of his own performance as Hitler in a (lost) 1933 piece for *Octobre*; it is true of *Fantômes (Ghosts)*, performed in July, 1933 by *Octobre*, who, along with other theatrical groups such as *Combat* and *Masses*, aimed to dynamically interact, as the program argued, with "your deep concerns, your hopes, your real life" and this, via "simple means" (cf. 2,1368); it is true even of the longer play *La Famille tuyau de poêle ou Une famille bien unie (The Stovepipe Family or A Well-Knit Family)*, a play rewritten for its 1955 publication in *La Pluie et le beau temps* and described by Artaud who witnessed its 1933 performance as "in search of a myth it is poised to discover" (cf. 1,1345). Referring to Prévert's theatrical innovation as a whole, Artaud speaks of "farces which are bloody critiques of bourgeois mores and ways of thinking", plays in which dream implicitly overlays caricature, where light emerges from shadows to "overcome the shadows of chaos" (1,1346).

Vaudeville, farce, the absurd, by all means; but never is there anything gratuitous in these plays and scenes Prévert writes, very largely for *Octobre* – though also in other collaborations (such as the short pieces he wrote for the dancer Pomiès). And although Prévert's work may be said to be one of "ideas" – he winkingly claims this in a 1954 interview with the journal *Arts* (cf. 1,1348) – one should never underestimate his sensitivity to form, to means, to theatrical and linguistic finesse. Prévert may be no esthete, but beauty is something he appreciated wherever he could find it, in any dimension of life; and his sense of rhythm, pacing, his economy of means, his inimitable wordplay, that superb balance of urgent existential purpose and uncluttered expressive ease brought to him some of the greatest creative collaborators of the century in the domains of music, song, film, art, photography. And the admiration of writers as diverse as Char and Sartre, Michaux and Perse.

1935 sees a continuation of this intense creative activity for and with the *Octobre* theater group. *Fantômes* is performed in a beefed up version. *Le Réveillon tragique (Christmas Eve Tragedy)* is staged at the Maison de la Culture directed at the time by Aragon who, in an article in *Commune* speaks of the play's youthful, mirthful and satirical vitality, its "cock-and-bull" skipping about, its crucially unmoralising manner, its intimate sense of Parisian banter and resistant laughter at the contradictions of life. "He [also] knows", Aragon concludes, "how we shall get out of all this mess" (cf. 2,1370). In June, at a large open-air celebration at Saint-Cyr-L'École, *Octobre* performs Prévert's *Suivez le druide (Follow the Druid)*, written a month or so before and already well rehearsed. A scandal erupts. Politicians want to know how the army and its chief officers can have been scoffed at for hours in front of the Officers' Training School. Yet despite this, *Suivez le druide* – of which no text remains extant – is performed again a month later in Villejuif. Early in 1936 *Le Tableau des merveilles (The Picture of Marvels)* is produced by Jean-Louis Barrault in an *Octobre* performance at the Maison de la Culture. The play, "adapted [by Prévert from Cervantes] with dazzling flair" according to an article in *L'Humanité* (cf. 1,1230) and praised by Roger Vitrac in attendance at one of the many ensuing performances staged in various locales, enjoyed considerable success and, as Vitrac writes, is "in the avant-garde of human preoccupations [and] points to profound changes" (cf. 1,1231). As ever, the play's means are minimal yet poetically critical, and what Vitrac calls "the tennis game of shared feeling in which actor and spectator lob balls over to each other for the pleasure of laughing and producing emotion" is very much central to this "popular" theater Prévert so relishes. A major show at La Mutualité shortly after gives *Octobre* the opportunity to perform again *Le Tableau des merveilles*, but this time along with two other pieces, the since unreedited *Printemps...été...1936 (Spring...Summer...1936)* and the short performable poem-sketch *Marche ou crève (Walk or Die)*, which, however, like *Le Tableau des merveilles*, will eventually be published in *Spectacle* in 1951. *Marche ou crève* had become the emblematic "hymn" of *Octobre* and it was performed/sung by the entire troupe. Here is its pivotal section:

> Toi t'es vigneron dans l'midi
> et c'est dans le nord qu'y a la grève
> Si on te laissait dans ton pays
> et qu'on te donne l'ordre de tirer
> tu ne tirerais pas sur ton père
> moi je suis pêcheur dans l'Finistère
> explique-moi pourquoi je tirerais
> sur un mineur du Pas-de-Calais

Tous les travailleurs sont des frères
Faut pas nous laisser posséder.
(You're a wine-grower in't South
and it's up North where they're strikin'
If you were left to get on with things where you live
and they order you to shoot
you wouldn't shoot at your father
I'm a fisherman from Finistere
tell me why I should open fire
on a miner from Calais way
All workers are brothers
Mustn't let anyone own us.) (1,328)

Socialist, if one likes, the piece's sheer creative verve leaps beyond ideology, counter-politics. It appeals to simple love and compassion amongst all people, a desire for freedom that refuses all external "ownership", preferring a kind of gentle though vigorously commonsensical anarchy. "Live free or die", as Americans might say.

Punchy and polemical pieces such as those performed at La Mutualité were produced on and off throughout the troubled year of 1936 in factories, striking department stores and so on. Despite this – perhaps in part because of it – though let us not forget that all performances taken together may have reached an audience of some twenty thousand – *Octobre* unravels, for financial and political reasons, in the fall of the same year. Prévert's *Bonne Nuit capitaine (Goodnight Captain)* reached the rehearsal stage but went no further.

THEATER: BEYOND *OCTOBRE*

From 1936 on Prévert's creative efforts redefine themselves and tend to proliferate. The ten years following the disbanding of *Octobre* are the great genial years of Prévert's involvement in the film world and they culminate in the publication of his enormously popular *Paroles*. Moreover, whilst generic and modal distinctions may be maintained between the worlds of theater, poetry, film, song and the art of collage that will also develop with Prévert, it is also important to appreciate how the energies generating these worlds flow naturally together in his case. So many so-called poems thus turn out to be theatrical pieces, and vice versa. So many of Prévert's songs are

121

adapted from poetic or theatrical or filmic contexts. Even Prévert's collages, which will be revealed some good time after the period of creative involvement with *Octobre*, are presented – as with *Fatras* – simultaneously with written texts of very great modal range: poems, satirical quotations, witty aphorisms, short dramas, prose texts of varying tonality, and so on. If Henri Michaux's encouragement, at the beginning of the war (1938-1939) is most cordially intentioned and seeks to offer Prévert publication of more "personal" texts, it is true too that Michaux probably is significantly underestimating the great "personal" creativity involved in Prévert's writing and imagination of filmscripts and scenarios of much subtlety. This transfer, or better, fusing, of the theatrical and the cinematographic – but also the written, the auditory, the visual – was moreover prepared during the *Octobre* years, not simply through Prévert's personally multiplying creativity, but because many of the actors and actresses of *Octobre* were themselves increasingly involved in the quickly developing universe of film acting.

Although, then, the war period sees Prévert devote himself very largely to his film writing and creation, Sylvain Itkine produces in 1939 – under the Occupation, and six months before Prévert's "escape" to the South – *Le Visiteur inattendu (The Unexpected Visitor)*, a play which, subsequent to its 1987 performance in Carros, near Nice, Arnaud Laster and Danièle Gasiglia-Laster regard as both a complex and penetrating indictment of bourgeois fear, inertia and decrepitude, and a farce full of subversive laughter. The imaginative elements broadly characterising Prévert's collaborations with *Octobre* thus continue to develop and, indeed, provide the "organic", unadulterated seeds that germinate so naturally in the many new creative soils now offering themselves to Prévert.

Theater, not surprisingly, however, will persist in playing an important role in Prévert's life, especially in the period from 1945 to 1956. In 1945, Roland Petit's ballet *Le Rendez-vous (The Meeting)* is staged with Brassaï's decors and photographic contribution, with Picasso's stage curtains, and with an *argument* – or plot or basic script – by Prévert. Two years later Michel de Ré produces, at the Rose Rouge, Prévert's *En famille (At Home)*, a typically outrageous microcosmic take on bourgeois clichés to do with parenting, a sharp, deceptively full playlet, over within ten minutes, yet lingering long in the mind caught between relishing the absurd and meditating upon its pertinence. (The text will become part of *Spectacle*, published in 1951.) Two years later again, in 1949, Yves Robert, again at the Rose Rouge, produces a show that stages two pieces by Prévert: *L'Opéra des girafes (Giraffe Opera)*, one of the "tales for misbehaving children" published in 1947 with Elsa Henriquez' delightful illustrations; and *Branle-bas de combat (Action Stations)*, a short play published first in the journal *Cinématographe* in 1937, then in *Spectacle*. Theater, "opera", narrative tale, filmscript: the lines separating such "genres" are clearly arbitrary for Prévert, who prefers creative freedom, generic and modal cross-fertilisation.

The 1950's continue to show that Prévert's writing is widely appreciated as multifaceted, generically supple, adaptable, and extremely theatrical in its essence even when not conceived specifically for the stage. Prévert's earlier direct involvement in such staging and performance greatly dissipates however. Thus does Michel de Ré produce *L'Addition (The Bill)* – a gleeful five-minute vignette allowing a restaurant client logically to demonstrate the impossibility of "adding up" eggs, veal, cheese, cigarettes and so on – in 1951. Thus does Chris Marker orchestrate in the same year various texts by Prévert in a Claude Kilian production performed by the Spartacus theater group. Thus does a Hamburg comic ballet production of the delightfully touching and yet vigorously uplifting *Coeur de docker (A Docker's Heart)* come about early in 1952 with music by Christiane Verger. *La Famille tuyau de poêle* resurfaces too, rewritten for its staging by Jean-Pierre Grenier in 1954, and two years later Maurice Béjart creates a ballet from Prévert's beautifully paced and orchestrated, charming and pointedly witty *Le Balayeur (The Sweeper)*. Other new theatrical work dates from the 1950's as well, work such as the ballet *Narcisse ou le puits (Narcissus or The Well)*, a reworking, it seems, of the shorter piece appearing in the 1951 *Spectacle*. From the later 1950's probably come also *Patte de velours (No Claws Showing)* and *L'Autographe (Autographed)*, ballet *arguments* equally, not only showing Prévert's liking for the cross-generic or multimedia creation, but also making clear the truly remarkable imaginative fertility of a poet able to pack so much, so delicately, so gracefully, so funnily, so perceptively, into such amazingly telescoped forms. Fantasy, rapidity, lightness of touch combine in both these pieces to theatricise Prévert's persistent phantasms of magical freedom, ease of transmutation, sudden discovery of and opening up to feelings of true, joyous love, when routine or melancholy threaten to dim natural vital buoyancy.

A final theatrical adaptation comes about, that done, in 1969, from Prévert's *Guignol* (1,555-73), which had been delightfully illustrated by Elsa Henriquez – to whom, one will recall, Prévert dedicated "Pour faire le portrait d'un oiseau" (1,106-7). The production was by Gisèle Tavet, in the little village of Saint-Jeannet, just outside Vence, in Southern France. Prévert's choice of this popular, working-class mode of theater demonstrates once more his anticonformist and free-wheeling creative thinking. The Punch and Judy tradition, moreover, is socially revolutionary, or better egalitarian, in its inspiration. It tends to laugh at, and symbolically "correct", exploitation of the weak and underprivileged, its elegantly economical aesthetics being underpinned by an ethos made to please a Prévert whose socio-political sympathies he did not again hesitate to manifest in the May 1968 upheavals in Paris. His *Guignol* thus wittily brings about an improbable socio-economic reversal, purely provisional, non-abusive though pushy, one of, for Prévert, purely phantasmatic power and emblematicalness: the one-week takeover by a poor family of the residence of a single wealthy bourgeois who, forced by the implacable logic of Prévert's wordplay to occupy the servant's quarters, can hardly believe his eyes or his ears and sleeps away the experience having taken pills prescribed for the alleviation of the pain of under-nourishment... Theater with a punch, inimitably articulated and conceived.

PHOTOGRAPHY: FROM RONIS TO BOUBAT

Prévert was not a photographer himself, it seems, but he was a great appreciator of the work of fine photographers and collaborated with several on various important book projects – beyond, of course, his significant experience of the moving photography of the world of film. Apart from the four photographers – Ylla, Villers, Doisneau and Izis – treated below, I should like quickly to explore Prévert's varying fascinations with seven or eight other photographers, this of course not only to reveal the intrinsic merits of the work at hand, but also to highlight the affinitary logic of such fascinations, the powerful echo in their work of preoccupations and visions at the heart of Prévert's own creativity.

"Les Mystères de la chambre noire" ("The Mysteries of the Dark Room", 2,624-6) is a text Prévert published in the journal *Quadrige* in 1946 with photographs by Willy Ronis, an uncompromising artist Prévert had known for years, given to photographing ordinary people and places, abandoning his work for the famous Rapho agency and *Time Life* and pursuing a largely independent creative course. The images obliquely evoked in Prévert's text, somewhat warped, and thus de-formed, re-formed, due to a technical miscalculation aesthetically exploited by Ronis, may be said to appeal for two principal reasons: 1. Prévert appreciates the spontaneous imagination of the photographer who realises the continuing, half-real, half-surreal beauty of the emerging frames; 2. the latter constitute a model for a modern creative impulse that, on the one hand, seeks to honor beauty in its most manifest states – trees, people, buildings, light and shade, etc. – and, on the other hand, knows that creation is visionary, imaginative, transformational, interventional and thus offers newness, provocation, difference in the midst of what seems like "well-behaved" sameness. The conclusion to Prévert's ever charming and witty text equally provokes those who flee modernity's differences:

Et ce village
ce village que le photographe croyait sage comme
une image
le voilà (sur une autre image)
Tout frémissant et qui s'agite
et se gondole littéralement
au nez d'une certaine sorte de gens
fous furieux de voir qu'il ressemble
insolemment et indéniablement
à cette « fameuse toile » de Soutine
ou d'un autre de ces vauriens
qui systématiquement s'obstinent
à peindre des choses...
des choses qui ne ressemblent absolument à rien!
(And this village
the village the photographer thought was well-behaved like
an image
here it is (on another image)
Quivering and worked up
and literally blistering

in the face of some people
crazed and angry at seeing it looking
cheekily and undeniably
like that "notorious canvas" by Soutine
or another of those good-for-nothings
who systematically and stubbornly
paint things...
things that look like nothing at all!)

Other photographers Prévert admires offer, of course, different takes on these two yet essential perspectives, honoring and basking in the real as it is given, and freely transmuting it in a photographic gesture that does not deny but rather complements such honoring. Günes Karabuda, for example, captures, and liberates, Paris via his images of the city; he is compared to the caliph of the *Arabian Nights* moving through the streets of Bagdad; his technique is "a simple matter of touch" (2,634), yet dream-like, ever available to surprise. "Life seen with the bare eye / the new eye / the only eye / the sun / in cahoots with darkness" (2,235). Peter Cornelius' photographs, as Prévert evokes them in his preface to the 1961 album *Couleur de Paris (The Color of Paris*, cf. 2,636-41) appeal not dissimilarly for their childlike marvelling at the world, their capacity to penetrate the backwaters and neglected spaces of the city, to offer new angles of vision upon the local, the immediate, angles that escape the eye and heart of "the tired city-dweller" – and, what is more, these are colored images, "so long denied by enlightened photography-lovers", yet praised by Prévert not for their aestheticism or the implicit technical prowess they represent, but because they are the authentic, felt "colors of Paris, of its secret music, its silent distress, its happy dreams, its songs of love". A third photographer to focus his gaze upon Paris, and with whom Prévert prepares the 1963 volume *Les Halles – L'Album du coeur de Paris*, is Romain Urhausen. Photography certainly is seen as a means – like Prévert's own text (cf. 2,642-7) – of recording and preservation of fleeting, even threatened life. But its caress, no doubt less blatantly nostalgic, less ironic than that of the poet's language, still seems to give the edge to what is loveable in life: the energy and vigor of ordinary working people, the cacophony and strange harmony of their teeming, pulsing activity, so simple yet so essential, at the heart – and in the heart – of Paris' vast collectivity. Photography quietly observes all of this, passes it on to the "passer-by who walks off, fragile and tottering [, watched by] a jovial, hairy, extremely old man, his gaze illuminated by *joie de vivre*".

Two other photographers should also be mentioned to complete this initial global sense of Prévert's strong appreciation of the very real power of what he already could see as an art form – like song and film – very much in touch with and available to everybody: Ohanian and Boubat. "Gitans" ("Gypsies", 2,661-2) is the title of a text Prévert wrote as an "introduction" to a 1968 Lyon exhibition of Ohanian's images of a people much admired by Prévert. Ohanian's photography as a whole is diverse in its fascinations: theater images in collaboration with producers from Chéreau to Vitez; scenes of people and their environment in New York, Rome, Algeria, Chicago, Venice, Brittany and so on. Prévert's text emphasises the freedom and roaming, nomadic life of gypsies – and implicitly Ohanian himself, for the poet perceives affinity and fraternalness at the root of these images. Just as "living true [is the] secret" of these utterly untethered people, so may this principle of truth be said to determine Ohanian's poet(h)ics. It is a truth, moreover, that is guided by a gaze of passion and energy seen in the eye of gypsy children through the desiring eye of the photographer. Prévert's text on Edouard Boubat, "Eternité instantanée" ("Eternity in a Flash", 2,663-4), was written in connection with a 1971 Paris exhibition of Boubat's photography stemming from his various visits to India. What delights Prévert here is, as ever, so charmingly yet pointedly indicative of all that really matters in the artistic, creative gesture, just as in everyday life itself – that other art form we so often feel, unlike the artist, to be beyond our creativity, our determination: 1. the perception of the interweaving of the immediate and the intemporal in existence, a perception that the photograph seizes, freezes, shows; 2. the seeing of what is, "the simple magic of things, beings, life when life is life, spared, out of danger, privileged, despite the harsh rigor of daily happiness"; 3. the energy, the grace, the soft and smiling beauty that life can offer, that people can be and live; 4. the concentration Boubat chooses, and we all can choose, upon the inconspicuous yet flagrant marvellousness of life: thus, instead of being a typical photographer-reporter of disaster, war, problem, Boubat chooses to be a "peace correspondent", chooses the oases of gentleness and simple joy, oases so commonly bypassed by us all.

PHOTOGRAPHY: YLLA, VILLERS, DOISNEAU, IZIS

Prévert created two of his early books in collaboration with the photographer Ylla: *Le Petit Lion*, which appeared in 1947, one year after *Paroles*, and *Des bêtes...*, published in 1950. The first of these two volumes (1,159-76) offers a series of Ylla's images of a lion cub in various improbable circumstances – in a park, in the company of rabbits and dogs and a cat, playing with a young boy, sitting on the lap of a young girl who is drawing, etc. –, the images giving rise to a typically charming fiction concocted by Prévert who concludes by saying that "the lives of plants, humans and animals are made up of reality, but also secret marvels and invented truths". It is Prévert's way of reminding us of the wondrous depths of the real, depths we can easily overlook, forget, even deride, and it is, too, Prévert's way of acknowledging Ylla's alertness to the grace, the ease, the astonishing natural yet mysterious beauty of a certain interchange between animals and ourselves. The images, like Prévert's prose text, however, do not appropriate the "meaning" of such creatures. It is, on the contrary, their freedom, their amazing fullness in themselves, their complex simplicity beyond our reduction, that incite Prévert and Ylla to focus upon them. Story there may be, but this is for the sheer uplifting, joyous fun of imagining with the same freedom and natural simpleness Prévert sees in (Ylla's images of) the lion cub and the other animals and children.

The second of Prévert's collaborations with Ylla (cf. 1,177-209) is couched in free verse, with its occasional spontaneous rhymes, and is orchestrated very differently: Prévert speaks directly of Ylla's photographic accomplishments; there is no "story" here: the text has a flickering coherence and continuity; Prévert is much more characteristically socio-politically allusive and he can mix up his forms of humor with the usual range of motivations; references to Char and Van Gogh, Jarry and Gorki pop up naturally throughout a free-flowing discourse. The following stanza catches something of these changes yet also stresses that all Ylla's portrayals here – of owls and swans, camels and cows, pigs and zebras, for example – convey the profound strangeness of animal life, its "distance" from us despite its equally odd closeness to us:

Des bêtes
comme des choses disparues et jamais oubliées

comme une étoile filante une blessure un baiser
comme un éclat de rire une source une chanson
comme des feuilles sur les arbres
des îles sous le vent
des hommes dans les rues et d'autres en prison
(Animals
like things long-gone and never forgotten
like a shooting star a wound a kiss
like laughter spring water a song
like leaves on trees
leeward islands
men on our streets and others in prison)

Ylla captures diversity, difference, the bizarre infinity of natural grace upon the planet, its energy, its beauty; and Prévert recognises this and articulates in turn something of the rich beingness of animal presence "with the same mystery / the same simplicity / as the waves of the sea the trees of the forest". The simple complexity or mysterious straightforwardness Prévert sees, of course, as being "without principles or attitude", without, that is, the moral and intellectual clutter of humans – though this in no way is held to diminish the remarkable lovingness and manifest other consciousness they display. Ylla's own genius, moreover, Prévert understands as intimately bound up with her own "childlike" capacity for loving and intuitively communicating with the animals she portrays via her images, "solemn beautiful mysterious and familiar". These photographs are part of Ylla's love of being alive, immersed in the primordial, unhierarchical, natural poetry of life. If we may be tempted to think at times – as does Prévert in the closing lines of *Des bêtes...* – of what is "horrible" or "absurd" or "disturbing" in life (and in the lives of the animals photographed), Prévert concludes, echoing Ylla's work, "it is never as horrible absurd unlivable disturbing as it is beautiful when it is beautiful".

"André Villers", as Prévert writes in 1970 for a Paris exhibition of the photographer's work, "is a cameraman of the secret reality of usual and oddly matching objects" (2,662). Obliged to spend, at the age of seventeen, some five years in convalescence and treatment in Vallauris, Villers will receive his first brand-new camera as a gift from Picasso. Above and beyond his famous portraits of writers and artists such as Aragon, Bunuel, Lacan, Le Corbusier, Hartung – and, of course, Picasso himself (cf. "Portraits de Picasso"

("Portraits of Picasso", 2,539-52)) – Villers' work orients itself towards various forms of montage. Thus, as Prévert argues in the above-quoted "André Villers est ..." ("André Villers is ...", 2,662), whilst the real is at the base of his photography, sheer creativity remains the fundamental motivating force. Honoring the real, loving its marvel, mystery and simple "thereness"– as with photographers as different as Boubat, Ylla, Urhausen or Ohanian – may continue as a subtext of Villers' photography, but the "smile" and the upliftingness Prévert discerns in it, stem from a creative impulse transcending and transmuting such directly portrayed immanence.

This is manifestly true, Prévert sees, in the collaboration of Villers and Picasso which gives rise to Prévert's own contribution to "accompany" their 1962 album *Diurnes* – the text is later taken up by Prévert in his 1966 *Fatras*. Here photographer and artist work together in various stages from 1954 on, stages which Villers himself describes as involving photography and cut-outs, montage, further cut-outs, further photography and so on (cf. 2,1001). However one might be inclined to intellectualise the process, the essential thing in Prévert's eyes is that "disfiguration", "figuration" or "transfiguration" are not frowned upon by nature (cf. 2,45). Human creativity, Villers', Picasso's, is like nature's: "natural", integral to all that is. And, as Prévert writes in another short text, on the occasion of the 1974 exhibition of Villers' photographic collaboration with the painter Max Papart, the sheer "pleasure" of such creative exchange is, perhaps, all that we need to focus upon – the artists' pleasure, and our own (cf. "Photographisme" ("Photographics", 2, 664)).

Prévert never truly collaborated with the photographer of the celebrated "Kiss", Robert Doisneau, unless we are to consider the sort of preface Prévert wrote in 1960 for a special issue of the journal *Le Point* devoted to "Bistrots" and featuring photographs by Doisneau, as well as self-commentaries by Doisneau. (The piece was titled "Gravures sur le zinc"("Bar Engravings", 2,120-22) and taken up by Prévert in *Fatras*.) Already in 1957, however, Prévert had published in the review *Caméra*, a "Portrait de Doisneau" ("Doisneau's Portrait", 2,632-3), in which crucial elements of Prévert's overall view of photographic and artistic enterprise become abundantly – and, of course, wittily, charmingly – clear: 1. Doisneau's work is intimately psychic, linked to his deepest identify, as Reverdy said of Braque: the dream-images of life register upon the psyche in their vastly varying moods and modalities; 2. the inner world (of psyche, imagination, feeling, dream and so on) thus comes to meld with the outer world , vibrationally, we might say; 3. Doisneau, whoever, whatever he photographs, is a "compatriot of life" – something much bigger than the nationalisms and constrained fervors we all know – and know, despite ourselves, to be limited, unfree, not fully connected to our true "life" energy; 4. it is because of this connection to a larger field of energy, this affinity for life, the "allowance" of life in all of its forms and manifestations that Doisneau can bring out, "from the most defeated, the most devastated of faces [...] an almost happy glimmer, a flash"– precisely of, within the subject photographed, this same connection to life's deepest resources; 5. Doisneau's photographic portraiture, not surprisingly in this perspective, is viewed by Prévert as "always in some regards a self-portrait"– again, somehow for Prévert, life is life, "Rolleiflex or Pandora's box, it comes from the same factory nobody ever has found".

The other text of note Prévert devotes to Doisneau, in the journal *Zoom*, in 1976, a year before Prévert's death, is titled "Transhumance" (2,665) and is inspired both by the photographer's images of shepherding and by the latter's attitude towards his creation of them. This point is well brought out by Danièle Gasiglia-Laster and Arnaud Laster, echoing Prévert's own emphasis (cf. 2,1360-61): if Doisneau, like other photographers Prévert admires, is a kind of "reporter" or "correspondent", he avoids sensationalism, his poetics being a po*ethics* of close, caressing exchange. Humanity, meaningful relationship outweigh always even aesthetic considerations, even though the photos of such lives as those lived by a solitary man high in the hills and mountains with his flock remain "such beautiful and simply astonishing images, and always [are taken] on the occasion of the Marriage and Wedding Reception of life's love and humor".

Izis, the final photographer of whom it is essential to speak, worked with Prévert on various major creative projects: *Grand Bal du printemps* (1951), *Charmes de Londres* (1952) and *Le Cirque d'Izis* (1965), which also involved Chagall. Of Lithuanian origin, Izis came to Paris in 1936, aged nineteen, the war forcing his departure from the city which, like Prévert, he loved for its teeming unsung backwaters and ordinary marvels. *Grand Bal du printemps* (1,435-82) comes about at Prévert's suggestion, unable as he was in 1948-49 to accept Izis' own invitation to offer a text for his *Paris des rêves* album appearing in 1950. Izis' description , in a 1980 letter to Arnaud Laster (cf. 1,1242), of the nature of the collaboration between photographer and writer is well worth our attention. "A photographer", Izis writes, "cannot illustrate a text: for a photo, the way I conceive it, *is not a composition, it is something one finds.* // Jacques Prévert did not bind his text to the photography (I appreciate this all the more), there is only an imaginary correspondence and his poems are self-sufficient. // I would show him photos, he would choose the images that were already in his possession; it even happened that he took out poems from amongst his papers and put them in association with the photos I had just brought him. When Jacques had chosen his photos he spread them out on the ground then gathered them up in the order in which they figure in the book. // I was happy Jacques had found what he wanted in my images, the product of my meanderings". As for Prévert's view of Izis, his text describes him as a "door-to-door salesman of images", a "musician" of creative intensity, involved in the "portrayal of things and beings that [touch] him". The emotion generated, moreover, Prévert feels to be reciprocal: the photographer is moved, as are the objects of his attention (because of this attention); and all of the photographer's art depends upon this exchange, this capacity to see and to feel what is being seen. Thus may the beauty of what is photographed strike us, even though poverty and wretchedness may be visible too. Prévert quotes René Char to emphasise that all of this allows for a generalisation of love, a making available of a love that, otherwise, would not have materialised, and this love comes about, strangely, even though the photographer Izis so often turns his camera towards "strange strangers" – how different it is from the lessons of guardedness and distrust we are tempted to give our children! To turn the camera upon the other is thus to embrace a "truth", a beauty and a love so easily "forgotten" – and, of course – it is at the heart of Prévert's poetics, as we have seen – a "joy" that is the song of life.

The 1952 *Charmes de Londres* (1,483-522) follows quickly on the heels of *Grand Bal du printemps* and, as Danièle Gasiglia-Laster argues, may be deemed the "second panel of [the] urban diptych" (2,1260) Prévert and Izis create together. To prepare this album – much admired by Charlie Chaplin precisely for its poetic-photographic "counterpoint"– poet and photographer went on a trip to London with their publisher, Albert Mermoud who delightfully recalls how surprisingly good the often misbehaved Prévert was throughout. What strikes one again is the freedom of association of photograph and text, the supple deployment of the writer's own image-ination, anchored in the photographer's images of the real yet transforming, narrating and relating to them spontaneously, loosely, with ease. The title of the album, whilst evoking the beauties and delights, the magic and spell-bindingness, as well as the proliferating yet pressured presence of London's many trees (*charme*: *carpinus*: hornbeam), also is an apt reminder of the precisely *poietic* nature of the Prévert-Izis collection: *charmes*, as Danièle Gasiglia-Laster reminds us (cf. 1,1261), equally may be etymologically rooted in *carmina*, songs. The old songs and ditties of old London, the new spontaneous adaptations of the city's street children, the "songs" of its many poets. But the "songs", too, that Izis the "musician" and Prévert the writer of popular lyrics together have created as *Charmes de Londres*.

Some thirteen years after the publication of these two major albums, *Le Cirque d'Izis (Izis' Circus*, 2, 652-9) comes out. Four circus paintings by Chagall accompany Prévert's own text, which, of course, is predicated on the notion of the photographer's work being a vast circus-like space of dream, enchantment, laughter, yet all possible emotion. (Izis' photographs follow Prévert's text, rather than being interspersed with it: in this way Prévert (with Chagall) may be said to present Izis and give greater focus to the photographer's own "circus".)   Prévert himself does not idealise or gratuitously romanticise, here or elsewhere. What is "true" and beautiful about the circus, as well as Izis' oeuvre, is however that they are, precisely, authentic places of life: their truth and beauty are in the contrasts, the tensions, the range of existential options, conditions and patterns they straightforwardly reveal and embrace. If "Izis' camera is a magic box" it is not because it picks out objects of attention advantageous to some closeted or decorative sense of being, but because it has the capacity to see beauty always *as truth*, and therefore in all things. Its "magic" is in an eye informed by the heart's belief in the photogenic depths of all that the eye can alight on. This no doubt is why Prévert questions the element of "control" involved in Izis' work. The poet prefers to see the photographic act as a spontaneous and intuitive act showing what "gives rise to dream, fascinates, moves or pleases".

Whilst far from Surrealist automaticity, Izis' photography arises from impulse, but an impulse somehow guided by a will to love and seek joy. A very Prévertian interpretation, but one that neither Izis nor any of Prévert's admired photographers ever contradicts.

SONG AND SPEECH

> C'est une chanson qui nous
> ressemble
> (It's a song that sounds like us)
> Jacques Prévert, "Les Feuilles
> mortes" ("Autumn Leaves,
> 2,785-6)

SONG: FROM FERNANDEL, CORA VAUCAIRE AND EDITH PIAF TO SERGE REGGIANI, YVES MONTAND AND MARLENE DIETRICH

There is no doubt whatsoever about the profound impact Jacques Prévert's written work has upon the world of popular music and song in the 1930-1965 period. The strange thing is that he wrote very few songs as such and most of this impact comes from a recognition by composers, musicians and singers themselves of the great pertinent and potentially vast appeal of his poetry, a poetry of at once emotional intensity and understatement, of expressive subtlety and transparency, of buoyant wit and an odd mixture of fatalism and bravado. Collaborations of many kinds, of course, take place, but Prévert's contribution remains significantly that of a writer, a poet, albeit one of great spontaneity and impulsive creativity and one reciprocally inspired by the enthusiasms and very diverse energies of those around him in the interwoven worlds of theater, film, music, song and – let us never forget with Prévert – those spiritual places of release and exhilaration: circuses, fairs, even the streets with their buskers and organ grinders.

In the 1930's Prévert's influence in the world of song slowly but surely sets in. Fernandel, in Marc Allégret's 1934 film *L'Hôtel du libre échange*, can already be heard humming Prévert's *Chanson de l'éléphant (Elephant's Song)*; the very popular Moulin Rouge and Folies Bergères actress Florelle makes, in 1934 also, the very first recording of a Prévert song, the vigorous and provocative *Embrasse-moi (Kiss Me)*, to be sung later by both Edith Piaf and Juliette Gréco; and in 1935 Prévert meets Joseph Kosma, whose arrangements will be greatly determining in the huge popular success of Prévert's songs. 1936 will see the delightful Agnès Capri sing and speak a range of Jacques Prévert's work live at the Boeuf sur le Toit. Her rendering of, say, *Les Animaux ont des ennuis (Animals Have Problems)*, with the music of Christiane Verger (written for the piece as long ago as 1928) conveys joy and fun, with her fine bright voice, yet allows Prévert's satirical twists to penetrate. Not dissimilarly, her performance of *L'Orgue de barbarie (The Barrel Organ)*, with Kosma's music, is in the classic popular manner, lilting, babbling, energetic, subtle in its emotional tone. The 1930's close out with three small but decisive flourishes: Gilles and Julien record for Columbia *Familiale (Family)*, Prévert's discreetly punchy antibourgeois and antimilitarist poem, which Francis Lemarque will also soon record; Marianne Oswald sings three of Prévert's poems, with music by Kosma, for Columbia also: *La Grasse Matinée (Sleeping In)*, the famous *Chasse à l'enfant (Child Hunt)*, with its great rhythmic swell of "revolutionary" fervor, and the typically socially provocative yet all-embracing *Bruits de la nuit (Sounds of the Night)*; Jean Gabin sings *La Chanson de l'homme (Man's Song)* in Raymond Rouleau's 1937 film *Le Messager (The Messenger)* – with its characteristically toned and quirkily cadenced refrain:

> Ecoute la chanson de l'homme
> que tu aimais
> et qui t'aimait
> Elle est triste, elle est monotone,
> elle est comme elle est.
> (Listen to the song of the man
> you loved
> and who loved you too
> It's sad, its never the same,
> it is the way it is.)

The 1940's witness a veritable explosion of this accumulating energy Prévert's work inspires in the world of popular song. At the beginning of the decade Edith Piaf records *Embrasse-moi* with her usual remarkable blending of vibrancy and sobriety. Tino Rossi, in Pierre Billon's 1941 film *Le Soleil a toujours raison*, sings *Tu étais la plus belle (You Were the Most Beautiful of All)* with great delicacy of performance and orchestration. In Marcel Carné's 1942 film *Les Visiteurs du soir*, four songs by Prévert are heard: *Démons et merveilles (Demons and Wonders)*, that Michèle Arnaud will later record in a soft, haunting, wonderfully lyrical rendering, and three others, of which *Le Tendre et dangereux visage de l'amour (The Tender and Dangerous Face of Love)* seems to symbolise both Prévert's emotional quizzicalness and his capacity for halting yet fluid rhythms, at once Verlainian and more freely modern. In 1943, Jacques Jansen records three of these songs he had dubbed in the film; the legendary Charles Trénet sings *La Chanson du vitrier (Glassmaker's Song)* in Pierre Prévert's film *Adieu Léonard*; and Germaine Montéro, who will record many Prévert pieces over the years to come – pieces such as the intense, rivetting, dramatised *Le Désespoir est assis sur un banc (Despair is Sitting on a Park Bench)* or the powerful, feministically self-affirming *Et puis après (Je suis comme je suis) (And So what (I Am What I Am))* – Germaine Montéro will sing Jacques Prévert at L'Athénée in Paris.

This latter song, with music by Joseph Kosma, also emerges as a significant element in the great 1945 film Prévert created with Carné, *Les Enfants du paradis*: the beautiful, mesmerising and self-assuming Arletty hums it – for an audience either already in the know or tantalised to discover its full rendering. In 1946, too, film and song merge in *Les Portes de la nuit*, where Fabien Loris sings *Les Enfants qui s'aiment (Children in Love)* – a subtle and typically provocative piece for which Juliette Gréco will later offer a fine classical rendering – and where Yves Montand and a dubbed Nathalie Nattier will perform the soon to be world-famous *Les Feuilles mortes (Autumn Leaves)*. The beautiful voice of Cora Vaucaire is the first, however, to record *Les Feuilles mortes,* in 1948. It is, of course, a finely arranged composition by Kosma, but Cora Vaucaire's pacing and range of power, her exquisite articulation, the vibrant intimacy she generates with such naturalness guarantee the magnificent response audiences gave her in live concert performance. At the same recording session she also sings the justly celebrated and charming *Chanson des escargots qui vont à l'enterrement (Snails Going to a Funeral)*. She will go on to record many other Prévert pieces – *Paris at Night*, for example, where her smiling voice enchants, and *Fille d'acier (Steel Girl)*, where her quiet intensity allows a short song to quickly generate its power, impose presence and close off with enigmatic abruptness. 1948 is also the year in which Yves Montand records the first two of what will be very many Prévert songs: *Les Cireurs de soulier de Broadway (Broadway's Shoe-Shine Men)*, with music by Henri Crolla, and *Les Enfants qui s'aiment*. The end of the decade brings considerable further creativity with Catherine Sauvage's various recordings. Hers, for example, is the vigorous, challenging performance of the *Octobre* group's "marching song", *Marche ou crève*, but she also sang tiny, bouncy, throwaway pieces such as *On frappe (Someone's Knocking)*, gave classic deep voice renderings of Prévert-Kosma's *Les Oiseaux du souci (Birds of Care)*, and offered beautiful semi-theatrical and charmingly articulated interpretations of compositions such as *Noël des ramasseurs de neige (Snow-Shovellers' Christmas)* with its mixture of nostalgia and joy and compassion. In 1949, too, Yves Montand records *Les Feuilles mortes* along with *La Fête continue (The Celebration Goes On)*, and the group Les Frères Jacques, who were to remain like Montand – and, indeed, many others – remarkably faithful to Prévert's genius, records nine Prévert poems set to music by Kosma.

The 1950's, which will see Prévert's position as a song-writer or song-provider reach its apogee, begin with a veritable bang. In 1950 alone we can note 1. the recording of the Prévert-Kosma songs from *Le Berger et le Ramoneur (The Shepherd and the Chimney Sweep)*, a recording involving, amongst others, Pierre Brasseur, Anouk Aimé, Roger Blin and Serge Reggiani – who will sing or recite ultimately a wide range of Prévert material of greatly varying tonality (*La Fête continunue*), the soberly yet intensely spoken *Pour toi mon amour (For You my Love)*, the provocatively orchestrated *Pater Noster*, and so on); 2. Claire Leclerc's recording of the songs from the film *Les Visiteurs du soir* and of a song from the 1946 documentary film *Aubervilliers* Prévert made with Eli Lotar, *Chanson des enfants (Song of the Children); 3.* Yves Montand's performance, in Christian Jaque's film *Souvenirs perdus (Lost Memories)*, of various Prévert songs: *Les Feuilles mortes*, bits of the Kosma-arranged *Compagnons des mauvais jours (Rough Time Friends)* that Reggiani will also later record, and, especially, *Tournesol (Sunflower)*, an energetic, buoyant piece with its fair-like context and children's chorus; 4. Les Frères Jacques also record these two latter songs, having been awarded the Grand Prix du Disque for their barbershop *à la française* rendering of *Inventaire (Inventory)*, originally published in *Paroles* (1,131-3); 5. Edith Piaf records, in New York, *Autumn Leaves,* Johnny Mercer's adaptation of Prévert's *Feuilles mortes*, still with Kosma's arrangement. The highly creative and happy collaboration of Prévert and Kosma comes to an end, however, in the following year due to a disagreement over modifications made without their accord to the cartoon film *La Bergère et le Ramoneur*.

In 1951 also Juliette Gréco makes memorable recordings of a good number of Prévert pieces – with music by Kosma. *A la belle étoile (Under Open Skies)* is given full orchestration – something that becomes more and more noticeable with subsequent recordings by, say, Catherine Ribeiro, Claude Nougaro or Marlene Dietrich (in her subtle and yet huskily explosive rendering of the celebrated *Déjeuner du matin (Breakfast)*) – and Gréco's manner is vigorous with yet shifting tone and insistency. Her performance of *La Belle vie (A Fine Life)* is upbeat, delicate, full of the poem's original charm, yet equally alert to its satirical bite, and *Les Enfants qui s'aiment* is given fine orchestration and a performance in the classic modern French tradition.

1953 sees the publication of *Tour de chant,* a collection of some fourteen of Prévert's texts put to music by Christiane Verger who, no fewer than twenty-five years earlier, one will recall, had written a musical arrangement for *Les Animaux ont des ennuis*. But the same year is even more spectacularly marked by Yves Montand's "mythical recital", as Georges Unglik calles it (JP, 1,27), at l'Étoile. A double album results from this live public performance, during which it is generally agreed that *Les Feuilles mortes* imposes itself in a hugely successful way. A year later Montand receives his first golden disk for the latter song, and, by 1955, Roger Williams and his orchestra in the USA had sold over two million records of their arrangement of the now celebrated song. In 1954 Prévert himself steps more forthrightly into the picture, recording for Philips readings of twenty of his own texts, accompanied by Henri Crolla on the guitar. This collaboration is rewarded with the Grand Prix du Disque 1954 de l'Académie Charles Cros.

It is interesting to take stock of what Prévert's own recordings represent and how, and perhaps why, they differ from the by now considerable creative interventions of singers of great genius and range. What strikes initially, beyond the fact that Prévert elects simply to read his songs and poems, is, on the one hand, a certain orientation in the selection of his material, and, on the other hand, the seemingly natural adoption of a particular tonality and rhythm corresponding to the selection made. Take, for example, the reading of *Chanson dans le sang (Song in the Blood)*, discreetly intense, beyond moralising yet pointed in delivery and, of course, theme. The rhythm avoids lyricism, sentimentality therefore even more; Prévert's voice, quick, softly staccato, echoes in tone and emotional implication that of Gabin in its mixture of in-one's-face provocativeness and plain acceptance of, presumably, life's "facts". *Le Combat avec l'ange (Fighting with the Angel)* shows, perhaps, the limit of Prévert's adventure with an albeit witty, but somber ironic intensity of delivery. The sheer – though always finally restrained – energy of voice and cadence compensates, of course, for a choice of texts frequently satirical and contestatary. Not for Prévert the brilliant charm, the bubbling delicacy, the sheer fun and fantasy of many other of his texts, of, too, many renderings by the numerous fine singers who loved and honored his work. *Tourneur de ritournelles (Churning Out the Old Tunes)* might have allowed the insertion of a softened tone, just as *Fête (Birthday)*, with Crolla's delightful accompanying entry, might have. The intense presence of Prévert's voice never slips towards such options however; the joy, the love yet at the center of his poetics come across in modified forms: compassion, attentiveness, an embrace of life as enigma, at best an object of his witticisms or ironies. His recording of *Étranges étrangers*, full of thought for so many feeling displacement or marginality, certainly projects a powerful and affinitary gaze upon the world, but its litanic rhythm without emotional climax or release, fights shy of more overt and brilliantly cordial expression. Something similar could be said of Prévert's reading of *Complainte de Vincent (Vincent's Lament)*: it is poised and, although the voice is strong and resonant, it seeks a deliberate evenness, a kind of intense *voix blanche* that conveys compassion but unprotestingly, matter-of-factly. There is, in short, always something of the *Barbara* tone and mentality in these readings – often of early pieces from *Paroles* – so that the space of engagement with the listener is filled with a quiet yet flattish penetrating passion, lit by only occasional brighter intonations or by Crolla's discreet and again rare guitar flourishes. This is true of the dramatic quick performance of *Il ne faut pas (We Mustn't)* and that given to the funny but pointed *Cortège (Procession)*, where Prévert does not opt for laughter or even softly conveyed smile – that is a choice left to the listener – although Prévert's somewhat poker-faced rendering does succeed in giving us a clear sense of the power and vision of his genial sweeping gaze upon life's swarming and often improbable human states and actions.

The later fifties see, for example, Nat King Cole singing Johnny Mercer's adaptation of *Les Feuille mortes, Autumn Leaves*, in Robert Aldrich's 1956 film of the same name, starring Joan Crawford; and Gina Lollobrigida, the same year, sings *Pas de rideau (No Curtains)* in the Prévert-scripted *Notre Dame de Paris (The Hunchback of Notre-Dame)*. 1957 is a significant moment in that Jacques Canetti, to whom those seeking to listen to songs written or inspired by Prévert owe so much today, sets up a new collection, Philips-Réalités, ushered in with fourteen Prévert songs by Les Frères Jacques. The Dutch musician Marjo Tal also does arrangements of Prévert which are published by Ray Ventura under the title of *Dix chansons de Jacques Prévert*. And in 1959, Brigitte Bardot comes close to singing Prévert's theme song written in collaboration with Crolla for Michel Boisrond's film *Voulez-vous danser avec moi*: feeling the difficulty of this, Bardot gives the task to a male singer.

Some high moments remain in the 1960's, but they are the icing on a cake that, funnily enough, Prévert did not particularly set out to bake: Edith Piaf records her inimitable *Cri du coeur*, dedicated by Prévert to Crolla, who wrote the music for it (cf. 1,897-8); Prévert, with Crolla on guitar, records eleven more titles, including the celebrated *Chanson dans le sang* with its terse, crisp insistence on the centrality of blood, pulsing, vital, shed, in the spinning and turning of the planet and its teeming lives; Prévert and Crolla combine efforts again in writing *Tumbleweed* for Marcel Moussy's 1960 film *Saint-Tropez Blues*; Prévert sparkles with the equally brilliant Edith Piaf singing *Quand tu dors (When You're Sleeping)*, live on Europe 1's radio; Serge Gainsbourg writes and records *Chanson de Prévert* in 1961; 1962 sees Montand continue his very special relationship with Prévert in recording a further album of fifteen songs.

Much more could be said, of course. It would be possible to explore the talent of Mouloudji singing the long-radio-censored *Barbara* or the fine *Bruits de la nuit (Sounds of the Night)* with the delicate orchestration of Michel Legrand. François Perier's remarkable live recording of the memorable opening text of *Paroles*, the corrosively witty (as Alain Poulanges writes), the linguistically expansive and liberating *Dîner de têtes*, this too would bear careful attention. And, of course, so many other fine singers and actors or actresses have performed "songs" by Prévert: Jean Guidoni, for example, with his husky, loping, punchy performance of *La Chanson de l'homme* in the film *Le Messager*; Sarah Boréo with her album devoted to Prévert's work, where in particular we might explore the modern, whimsical and whispered intensity of her *In memoriam* rendering, or the wonderful performance of *La Femme acéphale (Headless Woman)*; the paths of Jeanne Moreau, Simone Signoret and Gérard Depardieu have crossed with those, most plural, of Prévert; Manon's rendering of the famous *C'est l'amour qui m'a faite*, with its energetic mixture of Charleston-style rhythm and laughing exhilaration in a new arrangement by Jean-Marie Hummel, shows the very fluid potential of Prévert's work; Zette's 1975 album gives us Prévert in hauntingly penetrating, half-nostalgic (via the accordeon), half-jazzed mode; we could profitably juxtapose the delicate tonalities of, say, a Michel Simon (and Agnès Capri) rendering of *Petits pigeons (Little Pigeons)* in the 1937 film *Drôle de drame* with those, full-bodied, vigorously orchestrated, of, say, Catherine Ribeiro in the 1978 recording of *Câble confidentiel (Confidential Telegram)* and *Pour la batterie (For the Drums)*.

But, if one needed any proof that, despite his death in 1977, Jacques Prévert was alive and well and living in the hearts of so many in a "postmodern" era – how Prévert would have laughed! –, it could best be furnished by listening to the audience response to the performance, at L'Olympia, in October 1981, by Yves Montand, of Prévert's *Les Feuilles Mortes*. Duke Ellington, Frank Sinatra, Nat King Cole, Roger Williams and others may have brought Prévert's song to the attention of millions in North America; Montand confirmed it was still firmly implanted in the French psyche in the 1980's.

SPEECH: LITERATURE, GENRE, WORD

Speech, of course, is but the umbrella mode or category in which song deploys itself. And this is true, too, for all of Prévert's work in the worlds of theater and film. Texts, poems, plays, songs, film scenarios may be written, but they remain for Prévert *paroles*, spoken, speakable language. Their logic may not coincide exactly with that propelling the work of, say, Francis Ponge, but the aesthetics, and the ontology, of *parole* or speech shy away from those of *écriture* or written, literary language in various ways. Not the least of these – but what follows will anchor things with greater specificity in Prévert's own practice and conceptualisations – is the sense of the ephemeral, distinctly un-immortal nature of "speech". Its naturalness, too, is significant, as are its relative spontaneity, its impulsiveness, its aesthetic unpretentiousness. And, of course, speech is conversation, a fluid exchange with self and other; the very first text of *Paroles*, "Tentative de description d'un dîner de têtes à Paris-France" (1,3-12) makes this abundantly clear, as does any filmscript, piece of theater or song, and even Prévert's writings on or for artists, photographers or filmmakers are all articulated in this intimate, dialogic mode. "Speech", then, avoids abstraction, depersonalised conceptualisation, it engages people, including the self, with a freshness and an openness that people do, indeed, find engaging. Prévert tells us, in "Enfance" (2,252), of his growing habit of talking to himself; his friends tell us, too, of his early capacity to speak in great endless cascades; *Hebdromadaires* is the extraordinary record of Prévert's long conversation with André Pozner, a kind of live theater in which Prévert speaks with the teeming characters of the vast play of his mind, a text instantaneously "written" aloud, a huge collage of quotation from and commentary on his cuttings, his files, his memories, his impulses.

What then is "literature" for Prévert, what can it be? The short answer is that it can be whatever it wants to be, despite the pretensions and constraints some would impose upon it. "Would it still be the war of the gang of high forms against the slang of the lower strata?", Prévert asks in *Choses et autres* (2,282). Hence Prévert's common antilyricism, even though he can give himself to great cadenced expressions of compassion and tender appreciation. Hence his literary parodies, which, in the case of a Baudelaire, say (cf. 1,881), do not prevent a sensitivity to worth and authenticity. Hence, too, his witty dismissal of what he calls in *Imaginaires* (2,176), "the country squires of the realm of ideas [who] remain perplexed faced with the graffiti of the vagabonds of thought", *Graffiti* being the title of an important section of *Choses et autres* which begins, pointedly, with the statement/fragment "Beauty is called plural" (2,271). Just as in *Hebdromadaires* (2,898) Prévert argues for specificity and an anchoring of exchange in the real, and against generalisations that over-intellectualise and over-appropriate, so he argues in the literary context, in *Choses et autres* (2,280), for a "destructure of structures" (cf. *Travaux en cours)*, a deconstruction, at bottom, of all concepts and isms and quantifying formal or linguistic grills limiting art – and being. "Childlike, wild or extravagant, a strange language wanders freely whose words are remote-controlled well beyond the muddle of critics" (2,282): this is Prévert's reply to those who would reduce and systematise "literature", the only purpose of which, in his eyes, is the mystery of joyous creation and visceral release, to be shared with real people.

It is not surprising, then – we have seen at this point many examples of it – that Prévert's conception of genre distinction is utterly liberated and carefree, unconcerned with the categories and niceties scholars and intellectuals might be tempted to dwell upon. Speaking with André Pozner, Prévert offers, surprisingly – given his preceding words (: "Everyone has his or her ideas. There's a still funnier word yet: *concept!* Conception is always immaculate, often inoculated. There are things it's better to do than to speak about", 2,913) – yet with characteristic vigor, easy insight and spontaneity, the following definition of the "genre" to which he gives himself throughout his creative life:

> La poésie, c'est ce qu'on rêve, ce qu'on imagine, ce qu'on désire et ce qui arrive, souvent. La poésie est partout comme Dieu n'est nulle part. La poésie, c'est un des plus vrais, un des plus utiles surnoms de la vie.
> (Poetry is what one dreams, what one imagines, what one desires and what, often, happens. Poetry is everywhere the way God is nowhere. Poetry is one of the truest, one of the most useful surnames of life.) (2,913)

Poetry is thus defined far from the generic codes of non-poets such as a Propp, a Marcel Cohen, a Jakobson, a Todorov or a Genette or a Lejeune, who are inclinded to more formalising, modalising characterisations. Subtle as some of these are, they lack the sweep of Prévert's vision of the poetic which, whilst provocative for some, implicity equates the divine with the poetic – which is everywhere, in everything, psychic, visceral, deeply, mysteriously purposeful, multifacettedly "true".

The *poietic*, then – a global generic designation for Prévert – bypasses the need to bother whether what is written is best termed "Punch and Judy Show" or "opera" or "spectacle" or "graffiti" or "song" or "story" or "charm" or "letter" or "speech" or "hodgepodge" or "this or that". Prévert's writing may thus be considered either ageneric or transgeneric, beyond generics or simply heterogeneous and heteroclitic. Modes shift constantly from poem to poem, from stanza to stanza even. Discursiveness, a certain anecdotalness, tends to dominate, but it is never ordinarily rational or analytic. Farce, quotation, *feuilleton* blend in and out of one another. Comedy may slip into *outragédie* ("outragedy", 2,49), the fairy-like into *féerie noire* ("black fairy play", 2,287), the touching into the an(ti)aesthetic, the dramatic into the laughingly-seriously *antinéodrame* ("antineodrama", 2,306). If the only true "genre" is poetry, in that it is "everywhere", taking on all forms, all tones, it becomes of no matter whether or not we speak of poem or antipoem, neopoem or, as Henri Pichette called his own, "apoems": the *poietic*, the creative, knows no bounds, nor needs to know any in order to function, be, engage with the millions who, instinctively, appreciate whatever it is Prévert offers. Theory may conceivably follow creation, but as Reverdy argued (as, along with Breton and Bonnefoy, one of the great aestheticians of twentieth-century French literature), creation is what comes first – and, as we have heard Prévert say, it may be all that really matters (cf. 2,913).

What, then, of words themselves for a poet whose delight in them and extraordinarily liberating deployment of them are everywhere visible? In his charming and, as ever, purposive "Colloques dans un sentier menant à un séminaire de création" ("Colloquia along a Path Leading to a Seminar on Creativity"), from the 1970 *Imaginaires* (2,164-7), Prévert writes of them as follows:

> Les mots sont les enfants du vocabulaire, il n'y a qu'à les voir sortir des cours de création et se précipiter dans la cour de récréation. Là ils se réinventent et se travestissent, ils éclatent de rire et leurs éclats de rire sont les morceaux d'un puzzle, d'une agressive et tendre mosaïque.
>
> Contre les maîtres mots, les mots tabous, c'est le tam-tam des mots-mots.

> Et les mots sacrés se désacralisent et les mots
> secrets se créent.
>
> (Words are vocabulary's children, you only have
> to see them coming out of creativity classes and rushing
> into the playground. There, they reinvent themselves and
> put on disguises, they burst into laughter and their laughter
> forms a great jigsaw puzzle, an aggressive and tender
> mosaic.
>
> Over and against master words, taboo words, and
> there we have the tom-tom of the word-words.
>
> And sacred words lose their sacredness and secret
> words secrete their creation.)

A number of important points may be stressed here: 1. a witty, buoyant lightness – one could call it the sheer joy of wordplay – may be said to be the real purpose at the heart of Prévert's practice of language. Is he not most at ease in the company of fellow *satrapes* of the Collège de Pataphysique or those of equally spontaneous merriment despite all else: Vian, Desnos, Queneau, Duhamel, even Breton, with whom Prévert fondly remembers laughing till the tears ran down their faces?; 2. if Prévert believes in human creativity, it is certainly not with the hallowed, quasi-mystical conception espoused by, he believes, many Neo-Romantics, but a creativity residing *in* language itself. (If this might seem an incomplete argument on Prévert's part, Danièle Gasiglia-Laster and Arnaud Laster set it out defensibly: 2, 1053-8.); 3. words come to "play", engage in an interplay, can be released into their intrinsic capacity for free interplay, and thus, it is true, via the writer but equally beyond the writer, can constantly, spontaneously "reinvent" themselves, recontextualise, reimagine and, in a sense, rewrite their power and their pertinence. (Again, if Prévert prefers to see this as a process embedded in language itself, it is that he wants to move away from the notion of a profound separation between writer and non-writer: language is available to all and, for Prévert, "popular" language's vigor is the proof of a lexical creativity, a linguistic genius, in language that can ever surge forth free, laughing. self-transforming within us all – if we believe this to be so, with him.); 4. the laughter generated by the resulting linguistic "puzzles" constitutes both an aggression and an act of love: this is very much in line with Prévert's poetics and central to our understanding of it: aggression is the

146

explosion of received idea, imprisoning belief, the control and abusiveness that words may represent; words that break free of such bondage, that freely and laughingly query and deform, reform, transform, seek via such explosiveness, to love, to caress – the self, the world, the intrinsic freedom of self-expression, self-contradiction, self-invention that only free, laughing language can afford; 5. no "master words", then, for Prévert: better taboo language, because it liberates, permits the rhythmic, drumming, "revolutionary" (– *mots-mots* seems a clear reference to the Mau-mau uprisings leading to the independence of Kenya –) emergence of repressed being and truth, and because it gives to the reader no impression of a master-slave relationship dominated by the genial, enlightened author; 6. words, then, function innocently, joyously, laughingly, healthily, freely, when they shed their aura of "sacredness", the impression that the writer may give of an untouchable, superior, quasi-religious or transcendent grill of significance placed upon them, alienatingly, for the reader may feel dispossessed, cut off from access to meaning in words privately appropriated; 7. the emergence of a "secrecy" attaching to words has, then, nothing to do with the process of dispossession and appropriation generated by a "sacred" language: this is, rather, the unpretentious, strange, but generally experiencable secrecy intrinsic to any and all words, the capacity of words to foster, in us all, for us all, a profound feeling of their natural but bizarre, innocent and joyously liberating creative malleability.

"Colloques dans un sentier menant à un séminaire de création" adds a few elements to this fundamental poetics of word. The word "happiness", Prévert rightly notes (2,166), is one that is either suppressed or derided in modern literature, yet for him it is a "word" – and, of course, an ontology, an entire logic of being – absolutely central to our freedom, our well-being, our daily, minute-by-minute experience. We have to feel the pertinence of the word within ourselves, of course, but its absence or disuse or its abuse does us no service. Unsurprisingly, this whole text of *Imaginaires* pits the "believer" against the "misbeliever", the questioner of the status quo, with his disbelief, his freedom, his "miscreation" and, as a Denis Roche might say, his *mécriture*, his "miswriting". The latter is, of course, just Prévert's will, and language's delightful natural capacity, to deflate the myths, ideas and fineries of words "sacredly" intellectualised or aestheticised. He is brief, and of course funny, in his final dismissal of such a use of language: "Who overly celebrates the cerebral makes the prevertebral shake with laughter" (2,166).

In effect, as a later text in *Imaginaires* makes clear, Prévert opts for a "childlike" practice of words, "do[ing] within [words, images] what [one] wants to, for it's [one's own] business" (2,171). Such a practice avoids, in Prévert's view – there are important parallels here with Dada, Surrealism and contemporaries such as Michaux and Ponge – the "lie" that words can easily be made to contain. A slightly later text appearing in *Choses et autres*, titled "Les douze demeures des heures de la nuit" ("The Twelve Dwellings of Night's Hours", 2,258), praises "wild true and childlike language", for in such language words are "all the time reborn". The words of children and ordinary people, without pretension, constantly in play, are for Prévert, as he tells André Pozner (2,907), an act and a place of transformation; it is to their language that "we owe" everything; others merely "codify" such dynamism, never keeping up with it, never really at its "source", which is "poetry". Children throw their stones, Prévert continues to argue to Pozner (*Hebdromadaires,* 2,908), in the "swamps of imposed thoughts, constrained thoughts" and the images their language conjures "make people laugh, people who are slaves like so many people today, slaves to ideas, truths, freedoms, slaves to so-called abolished slaveries, new slaves in today's fashions". It is the "unbound, truly freed marvels" of speech, as he called them in "Les douze demeures..." (2,258), that Prévert seeks to live, to revel in, to encourage us to speak and read and write, without hangup, in the innocence of joy and love.

FORM?

Prévert, then, certainly is not – any more than an Yves Bonnefoy today – a poet to encourage any impulse we might have to study, analyse and systematise our findings with respect to poetic form. Why, in effect, might we be so tempted: to identify the secret workings of the text, its "magical" functional power over the reader; to codify according to some mathematics the very specificity, the originality, of the poet examined; to revel more appreciatively, with greater logical understanding, in the sheer aestheticism of the poem at hand? No doubt something of all of these would inform our motivation. A motivation yet, in the eyes of Prévert, nobly naive, missing the point of poetry's gesture.

Nevertheless – we might be inclined to persist in thinking – is it not true that, for example, a whole range of structural mechanisms are at the heart of Prévert's writing? The repetitions (with their variations), the anaphoras, the accumulations and lists or "inventories" as Prévert sometimes may call them, may they not be said – because so frequently visible – to determine in part Prévert's poetics/aesthetics? Is Prévert not known for his great cascading rhythms, with their now smooth now jarring or simply astonishing juxtapositions? Would it not serve us well in our understanding of the subtle functions of Prévert's poetry – and, of course, his prose, too, his songs, his theater, even his film scripts – to catalog the rhetoric of its (their) continuities and discontinuities, the cases of ellipsis, of anacoluthon, of hypallage, and so on?

Similarly, would we not better penetrate to the very heart of Prévert's formal "tactics" by combing through his writing in search of the abundant "figures of meaning", as rhetoricians would term them, that give it color and character? Certainly, we would return from such a mission, our arms, or notepads, full of metaphors, examples of catachresis, hyperbole, metonymy and synedoche. And an additional notepad would be crowded with examples of Prévert's celebrated similes, here compact, staccato-like, there elongated à la Lautréamont, centered around the eternal *comme* reenergised by Surrealist vision; or, again, we would reap a rich harvest of tropes of irony and allegory. And once more we justly could feel we were drawing ever closer to the center of Prévert's creative maelstrom.

Moreover, just as critics may pore over Baudelaire's orchestration of the sonnet or Perse's structuring of verset and paragraph or stanza or poem as a whole, so may we feel it is a valuable exercise to quantify, in Prévert, range of line length, average line length; to calculate similarly patterns of stanzaic length in relation to length of poem; to assess incidence of end-rhyme, and, very important in Prévert, internal rhyme; to note the relative tendencies to center poems, bring all lines back to the left margin, or switch into prose. And, of course, all of our formalising perspectives could be applied to the fairly frequently chosen mode of prose Prévert unambiguously explores – though, as we have seen, without the niceties of generic distinction.

Lexicologically inclined linguists, furthermore, would readily find in Prévert various rich veins for their formalising excavations. Neologisms are not perhaps frequent, but transformation and reformation and fusion of words are common enough. Epenthesis, apocope and metathesis all occur, all being part of Prévert's arsenal of, at once, satire and pure fun. And, naturally, one could hope that, by grouping the vast contents of Prévert's lexicon – with the assistance of computers that Prévert has a good laugh at (cf. "En petits morceaux" ("In Little Bits", 2,281-6)) – one could establish his/its "semantic fields" and, thus, take one more giant step towards the brilliant and red-hot furnace in which creation, Prévert's precisely, is moulded and tempered to its final form.

This process of mathematising form – a process which could be expanded to assess the (undoubted) pertinence in Prévert of, say, antithesis, apostrophe, exclamation, exaggeration, prosopopoeia, etc. – in order to achieve the goals we had originally set ourselves (: identification of the secret workings of Prévert's poetry-as-text; codification and stabilisation of poetic specificities and originality; a more humble, but still, paradoxically, rationally based appreciation of the aesthetics (and, as it were, anti-aesthetic components) of Prévert's individual poems and/or oeuvre as a whole) – such a process does seem to hold out much promise and as we accumulate our (very easily acquired) data, we can feel increasingly confirmed in the usefulness of such a formalising, structural and linguistic approach. So why should Prévert be so skeptical, so smilingly mocking even? The answer is to be found, I believe, in the definition Prévert spontaneously gives to André Pozner of poetry, and which I shall offer again: "Poetry is what one dreams, what one imagines, what one desires and what, often, happens. Poetry is everywhere the way God is nowhere. Poetry is one of the truest, one of the most useful surnames of life" (2,913). The poetic can thus be seen to leap far beyond mathematics, prosody, rhetoric, all forms of forms, in the eyes of Prévert. It may have form, if it is a text, but form is not its purpose, not its preoccupation, not the "center" we might have thought we were attaining to. And, of course, Prévert resituates and refocusses our search in fundamental ways that will render it difficult if not impossible to carry out. Instead of counting syllables or working out the mathematics of line and stanza, instead of assessing rhyme, alliteration and other "musical" characteristics, instead of cataloguing structural and lexicological quirks or modes of semantic conveyance, we are pushed by Prévert to explore poetry as locus of dream and imagination. And if desire – purpose, aim, strategy, yes, but then desire is so much more that eludes rational nomination – if desire is a factor, poetry is equally what "happens": i.e. its "form-ation" is not overtly linked to formal tactics, structuring and systematising consciousness. Its "happening" is thus free of form if we believe the latter to be controlledly deployed, wittingly chosen. And, on top of it all, poetry (: etymologically, doing, creation, making), Prévert feels, is "everywhere" – that is, in texts and not in texts, in the createdness and becoming creation of all phenomena. Reverdy argued similarly that poetry was not in words, but "between the lines". And Prévert confirms this disorienting/reorienting view by telling us that poetry is a way of naming life – it is one of the names of life, all life.

We are thus a long way from our diligent and well intentioned calculations of Prévert's caesuras or compound sentence structures and our meditations upon the supposed significance of such mathematised data. Prévert himself has pushed us back towards conceptions of what he is "doing", "making" – "creating" only if we remember his earlier discussed observations pertaining to the act of artistic creativity – that kick from under us the comfortable supports formal analysis seemed to be about to provide. Such analysis, then, will not allow us to understand what "poetry" is. The latter lies beyond all the forms it may assume – a logic Prévert generally espouses, whether referring to textual or verbal form, or to the (forms of the) infinite phenomena and gestures and "doings" of the world at large. The secret functioning of text/world as form is, then, not offered to our understanding via such an approach. Moreover, because the forms of language's functioning identified and codified via our formalising approach are, indeed, the forms (merely) that language may take, it is clear – again, Prévert's *texte à démonter*, his sample "text to be taken apart" by linguists (cf. 2,285-6), confirms this – that no specificity, no originality can be anchored in, or explained by, such identification and codification. At best, we can succeed in showing how language may – and even then, according only to certain descriptive/analytic conventions – be said to work. Prévert becomes merely an example. One can find every figure and trope in any text and, indeed, in the mouth of endless speakers we don't want to call poets – for we persist in clinging to the pertinence of our statistics, the value of what we so much want to be "proof". Prévert, in a way, will be pleased with us: he is the first to decry the attribution of creative genius to the individual; it is, as we have seen, precisely in language that for him such genius resides. I shall not belabor the argument, nor its delicacy: Danièle Gasiglia-Laster, again, writes well here (cf. 2,1053-8). One final deconstruction, however: to seek via analysis of form to demonstrate the beauty of a poem, is not only to misalign things in Prévert's view, but it also orients the reader towards an either dainty, somewhat prettifying, or more severely intellectualised aestheticism that the author of *Fatras* and *Choses et autres* can be understood as disinclined to encourage. The sucrose niceties, formally mathematised or not, of a poem / song/ spectacle / collage / photograph / story are not made to interest Prévert. If, nevertheless, by "beauty" a reader may have in mind joyous, love-driven, world-caressing energy, then Prévert's attitude would be distinctly encouraging. Still, the pulling apart of beauty's whole via formalising computation seems a futile exercise to discover just how "useful" poetry, one of life's "surnames", may be.

PLAY AND PURPOSE

Play – and the wordplay of Prévert is evident, both subtle and flagrant on every page, almost every line of his work – play, of course, is play with form, but it is always purposeful, meaningful, it always has purpose, profound ontological purpose. This, of course, is what Prévert is driving at via his, for structuralists and formalists, quirky and off-the-wall, but, for others, extremely sensitive and insightful, definition expressed to André Pozner in *Hebdromadaires* (2,913). Certainly such play, with its punning, its rich allusiveness, its deformations and transformations, its spontaneous juxtapositions, oppositions and orchestrations of all sorts, develops a polemical agenda of provocation and off-handedness, shock and strategic buffoonery. The purpose of play is what is at stake here. It is certainly not intended to create more mental or emotional confusion out of sheer bloody-mindedness, any more than it is centered upon some gratuitousness, a kind of light-headed giddiness. As Pozner himself remarks (cf. 2,857), Prévert "doesn't use [words just] to be funny but to make us laugh at funny things, sad things, to caress or to

152

strike". To play is to connect with life, to be pertinent, as well as to be exuberant (instead of succumbing to frustration or depression).

What I am calling play – wordplay, play with ideas, juggling and balancing notions embedded in language, throwing them wildly into the air, perhaps even not catching them, or, when caught, showing us new kaleidoscopic images of a world reworded, re-expressed – may thus often appear antiaesthetic, antilyrical, antipoetic. But it is play that, far from being anti – Prévert is right to laugh at those who "sometimes tax me with anticlericalism" (2,856), or antimilitarism or anti-intellectualism – invites us to jubilate, to be exuberant, exhilarated, to revel in the simply, joyous expenditure of our intrinsic, natural energy. This play leading to the joy of the release of our natural energy can, in Prévert's eyes, be achieved via the embrace of a spiritual and visceral freedom, a fraternity/sorority without exceptions, a language of high "heart" and not just high-mindedness. To adore and delight in what we are and all that is, without hierarchy or reservation, may be said to be at the root of Prévert's play. It is a high-spirited purpose to attach to speech. If it can hesitate in its step at times, feeling the pull of some Beckettian temptation or the temptation of pure "pataphysical" or *satrape* verve, we surely can understand this in a man traversing two far-from-"great" world wars. That Prévert's speech maintains such high energy, such a high capacity for resistance before so much that might have lowered both its purpose and its play, is a great tribute not just to Prévert – and, of course, language itself, he would remind us! – but to the intense energies and joyous, spirited passions of very many people he lived and worked with, or simply observed in his home-from-home, the streets of the world.

ORIGINALITIES

> ...quand je pense que tu aurais pu devenir
> un grand tartiste, un grand écrit-vain...
> (...when I think that you might have
> become a grey tartist, a great or-for...)
> Jacques Prévert (2,816)

WRITING AROUND PRÉVERT

To consider, if not to answer, the question of Jacques Prévert's originality or distinctiveness – notions in which he himself characteristically didn't have much faith – is a rather tricky undertaking. It is one, however, into which I shall plunge headlong, firstly with regard to Prévert's contemporaries and secondly, looking beyond Prévert, beyond his death in 1977, with regard to the teeming and ever-becoming canon of the past twenty or so years. Such an effort will, of course, confirm much that precedes, but it is my hope that is will indeed enable us to appreciate in convincing manner, and this despite the necessarily summary nature of the assessments, the decidedly unique nature of that mosaic of fascinations, manners and self-perceptions that render Prévert's oeuvre so powerfully appealing to so many.

Of those members of the Surrealist movement that Prévert knew well, Desnos is in many ways the closest to the author of *Paroles* and *Fatras*. Prévert's "Aujourd'hui" ("Today", 2,450-51) speaks – some twelve years after Desnos' death in 1944 – of the latter's love of life, their laughter together, their arguing, too, for much – happily – separated, differentiated, their respective brilliances. That, "at every street corner" in the course of such laughing arguments, Prévert and Desnos could together "drink... / to the entire health / of a scattered world", a largely European world between wars, signals a capacity for joy in the midst of ideational purpose that would last throughout Prévert's life. A later text, "Robert, Robert Desnos..." (2,466), read by Prévert in a 1965 France Culture broadcast, emphasises the latter's pacifist, truly life-affirming attitudes – Desnos, he suggests, "died against war, hatred, bloody-minded stupidity"– and also distinguishes between sheer, buoyant laughter, very much à la Prévert, and the "absurd", "not yet in

154

vogue" at the time of the friendship between the two poets. In effect, whilst appreciating the power of dream and the marvelous, the mental openness and preparedness to yield to the intuitive and the unrationalisable, that characterise the broad Surrealist stance, Prévert shies away from anything that might limit freedom, as well as those impulses that would tend to dwell upon existential problem at the risk of dimming the light of our ever surging exuberance. Breton is a fine companion in joy, a finely evocative thinker in *Nadja* (cf. 2,178), but a deadening influence in his magisterial, excommunicative ways. (Michel Leiris suggests that Prévert "had no really philosophical thinking. He was more inclined to poke fun at us and our commitments".) Not dissimilarly, the playwrights and "philosophers" of the absurd – despite the brilliance and wit of Beckett's *En attendant Godot* or *Molloy*, the sparkling and pointed fatuities of Ionesco's *La Cantatrice chauve* or *Le Roi se meurt* – remain in some important measure out of synchrony with Prévert's more exhilarating and ease-encouraging modes. The increasingly minimalist perspectives of Beckett in, say, *Catastrophe et autres dramaticules* or Ionesco's growing obsessions with death, inevitably disconnect from a Prévert who can write *Charmes de Londres, Arbres* or *Fêtes*.

It is not that certain affinities, here as elsewhere, cannot be sensibly argued; but Prévert's global mosaic remains more nuanced and plays more manifestly – *Les Enfants du paradis*, for example, sets a range of tone and sensitivity no other writer of Prévert's generation achieves – the full gamut of emotion and mode. Michaux, Perse and Vian, as I shall presently show, intersect in significant ways with Prévert's creative trajectory, as did Desnos and Breton; but what, briefly, of three other great poets of his time: Reverdy, Ponge, and Char? The author of *Les Ardoises du toit, Ferraille* and the posthumous (1966) *Sables mouvants* illustrated by Picasso offers a poetics of economy, non-anecdotality and relative textual closure which, for Prévert, clearly would have been too finely aestheticising, even though he would have appreciated Reverdy's sense of imagery (adopted to a degree by Breton in his first Surrealist manifesto), as well as his (not well recognised) aim, through art, to reconnect with life, with being, "consubstantially" as he put it. Again, Prévert's "popular" impulse, his eagerness to avoid theorisation of a practice he regarded as self-justifying, his delight in rooting poetry in document and event, his view, too – reminiscent of Breton's aesthetics of convulsiveness – that "the sublime is corrosive" (2,169) – all these factors give his work a distinctiveness neither Reverdyan nor Pongian. Certainly, one could maintain that Francis Ponge's poetics of *objeu* (obplay) and *objoie* (objoy) – given the text's supposed incapacity to be truthful or to truly "give" us the objects, the things, of the world – is made to please a Prévert writing *Fatras* on the one hand and, on the other, a poem such as "Et la fête continue" ("And the Celebration Goes On", 1,226). And Ponge's "abandonment" of the conception and practice of the poem as a place of absoluteness, "infallibility", as he wrote, aesthetic refinement and closure, in favor of a poetics of *parole*, speech, open-endedness, unfinishedness, seems again somewhat in line with the author of poems called merely *Paroles*. A glance at *Le Savon* or *La Figue* (or *Comment une figue de paroles et pourquoi)* shows nevertheless a significant gap between the two respective poetic practices, despite affinities in principle, and this is true equally when we turn our attention to the work of René Char – who, moreover, broke in 1950 with the journal *Empédocle* in protest over an article it had published distinctly hostile to Prévert. Char's captaincy in the *maquis* during the war would not, of course, have particularly impressed Prévert, for, if freedom was an absolute in his eyes, anything bordering upon patriotism ran the risk of falling into various cultural and ideological traps. The wartime *Feuillets d'Hypnos* would thus certainly have been read with ambivalence. The desire, the passion, the sheer energy of Char's work are close, perhaps, to the "corrosive" jubilancy of Prévert, but equally quite distinct. And if Char can offer us poems dripping with experience of Provençal smells and sounds, full of a will to caress a shrinking, often menaced yet beloved world he has known since his earliest days – in *La Parole en archipel* or, say, *Aromates chasseurs* – he can also veer off in a rather more esoteric vein that is foreign to Prévert's aspirations. The latter's "density" is neither, in effect, that of Ponge, "semantic", "textual", nor that of Char, hermetic, metaphorical, allegorical; it involves a playing with words as purely jubilatory as it is ethically purposeful, as full of (the meaning of) laughter as it is of any other agenda.

If the originality, the distinctive genius of Prévert shines forth easily when we consider his work in the light of Saint-John Perse's considerable and very differently genial oeuvre, it is not inappropriate briefly to record some broad affinities with a poet whose intervention was critical in one of the earliest publishing ventures of Prévert: "Tentative de description d'un dîner de têtes à Paris-France" (1,2-12), in 1931, with the journal *Commerce* (cf. 1,1010, Perse's 1949 letter to Paulhan). (Maurice Nadeau suggests that Prévert's "place is between Eluard and Michaux or, if one prefers, between Breton and Perse".) The poetry of Perse, from *Enfance* to *Anabase* and *Amers*, is both anchored in swarming perception, a sensual, uninhibited concreteness, a celebration of life beyond its contradictions and frustrations, and yet vigorously atemporal, fighting off the (only seeming) limitations of self in order to embrace the collective, the cosmic, the universal. Nothing is too banal to be excluded; all accedes to its strangeness, its wondrousness, largely freed of simplistic moralisation. And solemnity melds with marvel and rejoicement. If Prévert's palate is larger, more tonally shifting, and if the almost ritualistic, shimmeringly liturgical qualities of Perse – whether in verse or in prose – are missing in his admired contemporary, much remains in Perse that would have been strangely, obliquely resonant in Prévert's, it is true, punchier, more bobbingly carefree, yet more smilingly abrasive mind.

Between Michaux and Prévert there can be said to be many links. The former varyingly encourages the latter, for reason, out of a certain felt affinity. The latter often speaks of the former: "The adult makes ignorance silly", Prévert writes, quoting Michaux's *Barbare en Asie* (cf. 2,175); Prévert appreciates Michaux's insight in assessing the largely missing ingredients of European culture and literature: "wisdom" and exuberance (cf. 2,434-5); what he observes above all in meeting Michaux in the streets by chance, is his "simplicity", his smile, his "secret love" of life, of anything (cf. 2,469-70). And, of course, Michaux, Prévert knew, was a loner, a truly free spirit eager to explore and by no means addicted to poetry or language, despite appearances. There are certainly many radical or simply nuanced differentiations to be insisted on here, as we move back and forth from *Lettre des Iles Baladar* to *Voyage en Grande Garabagne*, or from *Fatras* to *Paix dans les brisements*, but Michaux certainly might have also put his signature to Prévert's statement in *Hebdromadaires* (2,919):

> La chose littéraire, c'est mon
> métier, je le fais bien, mais ça
> n'est pas toute ma vie. J'aime

aussi la rue ou la mer ou
n'importe quoi.
(The literature thing is my trade,
I do it well, but it isn't my entire
life. I also love the streets or the
sea or anything at all.)

Boris Vian, Prévert's considerable friend, also might have happily signed such a statement. But, as with Michaux, very much in Prévert still cannot be traced to any manifest source. The very texts in which Prévert speaks of Vian demonstrate the astounding inimitableness of their author, whilst, at the same time, they evoke what binds together the two College of Pataphysics satraps of the Cité Véron near the Moulin Rouge – the third satrap, on their shared terrace, we will recall, being the Préverts' dog, Ergé. The references are quite numerous, from those in the "Lettre au Baron Mollet" ("Letter to Baron Mollet", 2,816) or in "Bibliofolie" ("Bibliofolly", 2,177-8) to the more important texts such as the 1961 "Lettre à Boris" ("Letter to Boris", 2,458-9) or "Boris Vian", included in *Fatras* (118-19). The latter, a free-verse poem dedicated to Vian's wife, centers on a good number of qualities and tendencies very precious to Prévert and dynamically pertinent to any shared "poetics" one might seek to construct: Vian's "heartfelt" approach, his needed and prescribed liberty, the *savoir-vivre* he possessed (which, clearly, had nothing to do with social niceties and surface manners but represented a *joie de vivre*), the "realness" of his laughter, the fact that, like Prévert, he was a "true deserter of unhappiness". But the deep distinctiveness of such a text typically cannot be anchored in these observations, preoccupations or "themes", important as they are, any more than an analysis of form will reveal it. No, Prévert's originality may be said to reside in and develop a moving mosaic of many elements; here, for example, the following: the poem as a kind of *tombeau*, offered to the living wife, yet firm, unsentimental, delightful rather than solemn, and ever witty; simplicity of language and structure combines with a revelling in the ever surging opportunities to play with the latter, yet it is a toying with pertinent meaning; the portrait of so much, in Vian, that Prévert liked, carries with it lighthearted digs at bourgeois approaches to life; lyricism (Vian's living of his life "in the foam of days / the glimmerings of happiness") fits seamlessly with nonchalance; the shifting but relatively stable rhythm of the poem (and the deployment of its "ideas") is constantly offset by an arhythmic upredictability; the overall context given this poem of remembrance and celebration is that of *Fatras*, i.e. a mere quirky "hodgepodge" of bits and pieces, juxtaposed moreover with Prévert's equally quirky collages. No other poet or writer of Prévert's generation – perhaps of any generation – comes close to creating such a bizarre yet touching, utterly unpretentious, simple yet unclassifiable mosaic. And so one could go down the list either of those with whom Prévert had certain contacts, for whom he had even very warm affection – from Queneau and Camus to Artaud and Sartre –, or of those with whom there exists no proof of exchange or affinity/tension: Beauvoir, Sarraute, Duras, Guillevic, Mansour, Bonnefoy. In all cases it would be possible to draw up equations of direct or indirect relevance, as one saw with Ionesco and Beckett. ("The last story-teller of modern poetry", Claude Roy writes, riding high over generic distinctions indeed indefensible in Prévert's hyper-chiasmal oeuvre.) Joyce Mansour, for example, would have delighted Prévert with swirling free and often provocative deployment of a language filled with both sensual and "ethical" energy. Yves Bonnefoy's distrust of concept and absolutism, his privileging of the inimitableness of experience in the moment, his poetics at once of consent, celebration, and contestation, question – elements such as these are easy to recognise as having real pertinence to Prévert. But with all these poets and writers the real or virtual overlappings only finally serve to demonstrate the particular and peculiar global originality of a poet who, in *Choses et autres* (2,255) can write:

MALGRÉ MOI...

Embauché malgré moi dans l'usine à idées
j'ai refusé de pointer
Mobilisé de même dans l'armée des idées
j'ai déserté
Je n'ai jamais compris grand-chose
Il n'y a jamais grand-chose
ni petite chose
Il y a *autre chose*.

Autre chose
c'est ce que j'aime qui me plaît
et que je fais.

    (IN SPITE OF MYSELF...

Given a job in spite of myself in the ideas factory
I refused to clock in
Mobilised likewise in the ideas army
I deserted
I have never understood much
There never is much
or little
There is *something else*.

Something else
is what I like and find pleasure in
and do.)

WRITING BEYOND PRÉVERT

"Beauty", writes Prévert in a telling poem from *Fatras* (2,62), "Often I use your name / and I work at publicising you / I'm not in charge / Beauty / I'm your employee". And one could argue similarly that Prévert, whilst having no prerogative understanding or control over such matters, is a pretty exemplary "employee" not only of beauty but of love and joy. To be in their employ, of course, is to choose to celebrate life over the "horrors", the "absurdity" and the "unlivableness" that Prévert knows threaten such a choice (cf. 1,209). And, at bottom, such a choice represents an instinctive understanding that literature, the very activity that allows a wide and popular "publicising" of beauty and joy and love of life, always finally plays, must play, second fiddle to primary experience. *Fatras* (2,61) again confirms this with lapidary wit:

J'aime mieux
        tes lèvres
que mes livres
(I prefer
        your lips
to my books).

160

To cast one's eye around the contemporary literary, and especially poetic, scene certainly allows us to see the persistence of something of this relatively distinctive cluster of impulses – and we should not forget that the pursuit of the "sublime" can entail a certain edge or "corrosiveness" in Prévert's estimation (2,69); that desire, involving choice, also means refusal. Feminist writers such as Hélène Cixous or Chantal Chawaf, Jeanne Hyvrard or Monique Wittig, can, in radically different ways and *toutes proportions gardées*, set their sights on the recognition and accomplishment of very much for us all: the beauty of difference; the love that is creatable within us if we but choose it; the simple, sensual, intellectual joy that can result from choosing life over our mortiferous actions and attitudes; and so on. These feminists could only be amazed and delighted to read one of Prévert's most powerful social critiques, the yet beautifully life-affirming and woman-affirming "La Femme acéphale" ("The Headless Woman", 2,364-84). And, of course, here seems to be the rub, for today's writers, feminist or not: how, in a post-Holocaust, but also postcolonial, broadly "postmodern" climate, does the writer unblinkingly disseminate a literature of beauty, love, joy and affirmation of life? The problem, naturally, posed itself for Prévert and the answer, now as then, is at bottom simple: what do we want, what do we truly desire? The challenge remains great, however, for the temptation is to dwell upon what is observable now – this was, after all, a significant tactic of Prévert's: the *fait divers*, the document, his endless files constantly dipped into in his conversations with André Pozner. Thus can Chantal Chawaf give us *Le Manteau noir* and not just the exhilarating cascades of self-rediscovery in contact with the earth's beauties; thus can Monique Wittig put us, literally, through the "hell" of *Virgile, non*, on the way to a glimpse of "paradise"; thus can Jeanne Hyvrard give us the terrors of *La Baisure* which, yet, is underpinned by utopian passion. Yet it remains that women such as these, or others such as Liliane Atlan in *Les Passants* with its remarkable poetics of "praise" in the aftermath of the Sho'ah devastation, come close to writing in that rare spirit of upliftment and aspiringly unconditional, natural love that would seek to drive the work of Prévert, in conjunction with its smiling and at times riotous exposures.

In Prévert's instinctive inclination to privilege raw experience, the ebb and flow of emotion in the moment, the profound pertinence of ephemerality and its apparent ordinariness, we might readily see the basis of an argument linking his work in a variety of ways to that of a number of poets and other writers of the past twenty years. Yves Bonnefoy's oeuvre has already been evoked, of course, and one could mention that of Philippe Jaccottet. The recent writing of five younger poets such as Yves Leclair, with his *L'Or du commun*, Jean-Claude Pinson with *Laïus au bord de l'eau*, or Marie-Claire Bancquart with *Dans le feuilletage de la terre*, also confirms that a deep appreciation of the wonders and glories of the fleeting and the fragile remains very much alive today in the midst of much pure intellectualism or blatant skepticism. Much, of course, needs nuancing here, from author to author and with regard to Prévert's own specificities. In particular one would want to insist on Prévert's dubiousness – emanating from his privileging of experience and life's becoming and a consequent unnameableness attaching to it – with regard to language's conceptualisations and artificial structurings. The song of nightingales, he tells André Pozner, "is what it is", the rest being "nightingale language demonstrated by scholars with keys" (2,868). Again, we are very close to aspects of Bonnefoy's work, although the author of the 1983 *La Présence et l'image* recognises the role of the conceptual – i.e., for him, (the prestige of) language and its rationalising structures – and its possible harmonisation with "presence", via a "conquering of image in image".

Prévert's wariness of all systematisation is matched undoubtedly by writers as radically different as André du Bouchet, Marguerite Duras and Alain Robbe-Grillet, and, of course, we could argue, with philosophers such as Blanchot and Adorno, that the poetic and the artistic, whatever their modal particularities, veer away from the (Aristotelian or other) "poetics", or order, we might seek to lay upon them so as to bring them back within the organised, socialised, normalising – conceptualising, intellectually rationalising – confines of the City or the Republic. What retains the attention of Prévert is thus never Man, but always this man or that woman, that child (cf. 2,870). His view of intelligence, he writes in "La Sagesse ou les poux dans la tête" ("Wisdom or Headlice", 2,943), is that it is "a sickness, a virus, and the intelligentsia the secret society of those most afflicted". The heart ever takes it over the head, for intelligence so easily blinds itself to the strangeness of existence, its ordinary beauties, its dazzling paradoxes, a deep principle of love far more worthy of our attention – again Le Clézio can figure eloquently such polarities, as may poets of extreme subtlety and (this time) felt wisdom, Heather Dohollau, Jacqueline Risset. Prévert, witty as always, puts it this way in one of his graffiti from *Choses et autres* (2,277): "Lots of books today, when we open them like an oyster we find merely cultured pearls". His worst fear – writers as distinct as Beckett and Dupin, Herlin and Prigent share the feeling – would center around becoming a "grey tartist, a great or-for" (2,816), for this could spell a vanity – both a pride and a futility – that only his jubilancy, his spurting wholesome laughter, his will for joy save him from.

If these latter characteristics constitute a significant element of Prévert's originality, they have not proved easy to emulate, even if, as André Laude firmly argues, Prévert "has done more than anyone else for poetry, for its modern adventures". A Jean-Claude Pinson seeks that balance of social sensitivity and buoyancy, observation and exhilaration; a Patrick Chamoiseau can rise smiling, exuberant in the midst of old ruin and regret; a Salah Stétié can run the gamut of consciousness and tone in a shimmering display of psychic and emotional energy. Prévert's special place of meditation is one eschewing definition, program, the idea of writing even as mediation. His delightful 1973 text on the painter and writer Marcel Jean, "Eaux fortes" ("Etchings"), reveals much of Prévert's refusal of isms and abstraction, category and what he deems to be idle intellectualisation. His final remarks merely argue that "[Marcel Jean] is the way he is, that is to say the way he doesn't know what he is, intuiting himself, going astray, finding himself again, writing, drawing, engraving or painting, but what is roughly sure are his honest and childlike personal papers" (2,602). Originality indefinable, turning, shifting, so deeply personal and beyond form and formulation... Marcel Jean liked as a whole, individual person, unrepeatable, irreducible to our dreamed computerised statistics and structures (cf. 2,345)... To have preferred, so often in consequence, the *fait divers*, the observed street scene, the lived and inconspicuous moment, only however constitutes an original feature of Prévert's poetics to the degree that it combines with other characteristic orientations and fascinations, and to the extent that Prévert sees the pertinence thereof as blinding, there but dazzlingly so, indisputable yet of uncertain meaning – like a tree, a shared glance, a kiss (in, say, *Quai des brumes*). Such preference for the barely sayable, yet paradoxally flagrant mortality that Prévert sees as our point of fragile anchorage, resistant to pure notionality, "discarnate" cerebralness – such preference certainly persists in varying shape and form in those writers we have mentioned to date or in others such as Pascal Commère (: the refusal of theorising in the writing of the rich ordinariness of a "consigned world", in, for example, *De l'humilité du monde chez les bousiers)*, Sylvie Germain (: the sweep of mortal contrast and paradox portrayed beyond attribution or recrimination, in, say, *Jours de colère*), Françoise Hàn (: the tensions of the lived and the observed, yet a sense of strange jubilancy despite the felt upheavals that can draw her socio-political pen, in, for example, *Une fête même au creux du sombre*), Claude Simon even (: his resistance to theory, his privileging of the teeming, fascinating concreteness, "there-ness" of our physical world and the strange mental patterns that weave our individual and collective being in and out of this unspeakable-even-if-endlessly-described world).

This consciousness that is Prévert's of the openness of life's deep meanings, their unfinishedness, their endless becoming and unfinishableness, and, it naturally follows, the utter relativity – despite its energy, its invigoratingness – of our speech, our *parole* – such consciousness, then, is closely tied to those originalities and specificities belonging to Prévert. If they may be said to front upon a sense of the absurd that we can see persist today in writers as diverse again as Marie Redonnet, Liliane Giraudon or Marie Ndiaye, they pull themselves loose from such comparisons via their either implicit or explicit insistence upon our (existentialist) power of choice, self-assumption, and the felt exhilaration (– an element remote from existentialism's sobrieties –) of such self-liberation. The so-called relativity of our speech, predicated on factors such as not-knowing, ephemeralness, enigma, produces in Prévert far less the sense of futility or the tragic so characteristic of many contemporaries, but rather a new-found liberty, a joy emanating from it, and, above all, a return to the world, the quotidian. Language thus becomes for Prévert the messenger of its own jubilant, raucous return to non-language: to presence, to direct, lived experience, to the rich hum, even hum-drum, of our life's minute-by-minute intensities. Prévert's originality always involves a subversiveness first and foremost focussed upon its own conceivable pretentiousness; but it undercuts itself via a process of self-energising exuberance that invites us to relive the world anew, as a place of improbable but feasible joy and love. René Gilson has spoken eloquently along these lines. Prévert's ironies, thus, are not defeatist; his creative specificity entails passion, compassion and vision. Even Beckett's lacerations contain the seeds of such reversal, though clearly less developed (: in *Molloy*, for example, Moran's surging, visceral passionate fascination at the thought of spending his life studying (: *studium*: enthusing over) his bees). Chamoiseau, again, can revel in the exquisite counter-history his *Texaco* narrative can generate, the narration-now taking it powerfully and energetically, genially, over the language of the other, long-dominating, tenderly and wittily shrugged off. Freedom is the name of such originality, freedom from one's own melancholies and cynicisms first of all. A freedom that does not submit to what, in *Imaginaires*, Prévert calls "the gloomy norms of a world in which the Worldly have forever sought in vain to pull down Earthlings below ground-level" (2,197)... A lack of submission that opens us up to the "countless wild images of life outside [of these gloomy norms]" (2,197)...

Prévert's will for non-conformity is not hollow; it endeavors to delight, unapologetically, in being who he feels he truly is, in all innocence, in all simplicity, beyond (self-)constraint. Such "originalities" as may emerge thus lack any project of aesthetic, conceptual or platitudinously moral, ethical revolution and subsequent stabilisation. Rather do they flow freely, ideationally, emotionally and generically. Prévert's originalities are transgressive in that they are shifting, ever transmuting, transgeneric, now lyrical, now vaudevillesque; now sweeping, now throwaway; now cogent and cutting, now utterly relaxed and irresistibly charming. *Is* there anyone writing today with the range of tone and form, mode and genre, to compare to that which characterises Prévert's oeuvre? Certainly there are considerable writers over the past thirty years with oeuvres that will endure and that possess breadth and great mutant energy. Yet an Yves Bonnefoy or a Michel Deguy, for all their multifocussed attentiveness, possess a relative constancy of mode and a subset of perspectives that remain at some distance from Prévert via their at times paradoxical conceptualisations and theorisings. And if an André du Bouchet has largely steered away from such refinements, his equally powerful and concentrated work chooses modes of openness, aeration and (self-)contestation that seem to leave little trace of Prévert's smiling or quirky playfulness. Could one turn to Perec, say, or Tournier, to fill such gaps? Perhaps, yet other differences loom larger as we draw such affinities; and, for various other reasons, the admirable emotional, sensual wealth in Le Clézio's today large oeuvre, its ecological, social and psychical sensitivities, its lived knowing of much that is essential to our individual and collective well-being – whilst much of this could be seen in affinity with Prévert, much else, tonally and generically is not – nor need it be, of course – in line with what, for example, *Fatras* or *La Femme acéphale* from *Choses et autres* relentlessly, punchily, wittily convey. Hélène Cixous, certainly, has produced an extraordinarily diverse, poignant and pointed body of felt and lived work. If her avenues of pursuit again do not especially coincide with Prévert's, there are, as with Le Clézio, factors of great interpertinence, of beautifully different sameness.

And so one could go on, seeking yet not finding the dreamed fit of originalities, specificities, with very fine writers such as Edouard Glissant or Tahar Ben Jelloun, with Jacques Chessex or Maryse Condé, with Jacques Ferron or Antonine Maillet, with Marie-Claire Blais or Régine Detambel. Some of these alignments are less probable than others, it goes without saying, though all can yield valid and fascinating continuities and interweavings. The sheer, swarming transgenericalness of Prévert, his multiplying modal and tonal manner, his determined belief in the power of exhilaration, joy, love and simple (though always wittily subtle) straightforwardness and common sense, these qualities make him a poet and a human being delightfully inimitable, endearingly unique. He would have yet rejoiced today in reading a good deal of fine work in not inconsiderable sympathy with his originalities. That, it seems to me, is a happy affair, for, as any bookstore can show, Prévert remains equally today, amongst what he might have called his "post-contemporaries", a choice very much of the people.

SELECTED BIBLIOGRAPHY

PRIMARY SOURCES

Oeuvres complètes, I. Ed. Danièle Gasiglia-Laster and Arnaud Laster. Paris: Pléiade, 1992.

Oeuvres complètes, II. Ed. Danièle Gasiglia-Laster and Arnaud Laster. Paris: Pléiade, 1996.

Paroles. Paris: Le Point du Jour, 1945, 1947; Paris: Gallimard, 1949; Coll. Folio, 1972.

Le Petit Lion. Paris: Arts et métiers graphiques, 1947. Photographs by Ylla.

Des bêtes.... Paris: Gallimard, 1950. Photographs by Ylla.

Spectacle. Paris: Gallimard, 1951; Coll. Folio, 1974.

Grand bal du printemps. Lausanne: La Guilde du Livre, 1951. Photographs by Izis. Coll. Folio, 1978 (with *Charmes de Londres*).

Charmes de Londres. Lausanne: La Guilde du Livre, 1952. Photographs by Izis. Coll. Folio, 1978.

Lettres des Iles Baladar. Paris: Gallimard, 1952. Drawings by André François.

Guignol. Lausanne: La Guilde du Livre, 1952. Illustrations by Elsa Henriquez. Coll. Enfantimages, 1978.

L'Opéra de la lune. Lausanne: La Guilde du Livre, 1953. Images by Jacqueline Duhême; music by Christiane Verger. Coll. Folio Benjamin, 1986.

Lumières d'homme. Paris: G.L.M., 1966.

La Pluie et le beau temps. Paris: Gallimard, 1955. Coll. Folio, 1978.

Histoires et d'autres histoires. Paris: Gallimard, 1963.

Fatras, Paris: Gallimard, 1966. With fifty-seven collages by Prévert. Coll. Folio, 1977.

Arbres. Paris: Edns de la Galerie D'Orsay, 1967. With engravings by Georges Ribemont-Dessaignes. Coll. Blanche, Gallimard, 1976.

Imaginaires. Geneva: Skira, 1970. Coll. Les Sentiers de la Création. With various collages by Prévert.

Fêtes. Paris: Maeght, 1971. With seven etchings by Alexander Calder.

Choses et autres. Paris: Gallimard, 1972; Coll. Folio, 1975.

Le Jour des temps. Paris: Galerie Bosquet et Jacques Goutal Darly, 1975. With engravings by Max Papart.

[Textes divers (1929-1977)] in *Oeuvres complètes, II*. Paris: Pléiade, 1996, 397-954. Presented by Arnaud Laster and Danièle Gasiglia-Laster. Contains a large number of usually compact texts on art (Picasso, Braque, Miró, Bauer, Fromanger, Jorn, Charbonnier, Vasarely, Vilato, Magritte, etc.), literature, photography (Ronis, Doisneau, Cornelius, Urhausen, Boubat, Izis, Ohanian, Villers, etc.), cinema, television, theater, song, current affairs, etc., and various other texts, including *Hebdromadaires*.

Hebdromadaires. Paris: Guy Authier, 1972. Exchanges with André Pozner. Coll. Folio, 1974, 1987 (enlarged edition).

Joan Miró. Paris: Maeght, 1956. With a text also by Georges Ribemont-Dessaignes and Miró reproductions.

Portraits de Picasso. Milano: Muggiani, 1959. With photographs by André Villers.

Varengeville. Paris: Maeght, 1968. With illustrations by Braque.

Couleur de Paris. Lausanne: Edita, 1961. With photographs by Peter Cornelius.

Les Halles – L'Album du coeur de Paris. Paris: Edns des Deux-Mondes, 1963. With photographs by Romain Urhausen.

Le Cirque d'Izis. Monte-Carlo: André Sauret, 1965. With four originals by Chagall and photographs by Izis (Bidermanas).

Collages. Paris: Gallimard, 1982. Preface by Philippe Soupault and texts by André Pozner.

Attention au Fakir! suivi de Textes pour la scène et l'écran. Ed. André Heinrich. Paris: Gallimard, 1995.

Soleil de nuit. Paris: Gallimard, 1980. Ed. Arnaud Laster, with Janine Prévert. Coll. Folio, 1989.

La Cinquième Saison. Paris: Gallimard, 1984. Ed. Arnaud Laster and Danièle Gasiglia-Laster, with Janine Prévert.

Blood and Feathers. Selected Poems of Jacques Prévert. Translations by Harriet Zinnes. Mt. Kisco, New York: Moyer Bell, 1993.

SECONDARY SOURCES

Andry, Marc. *Jacques Prévert*. Paris: Edns de Fallois, 1994. Biographical, anecdotal, atmospheric evocation.

Baker, William E. *Jacques Prévert*. New York: Twayne. TWAS 24, 1967. Important early global study.

Bataille, Georges. "De l'âge de pierre à Jacques Prévert", *Critique*, avr-sept 1946, 195-214.

Bergens, Andrée. *Jacques Prévert*. Paris: Edns Universitaires, 1969. A useful, concise early study of form and theme.

Bishop, Michael. "Jacques Prévert et la photographie", *Antemnae*, 1, Dec. 1999, 1-12.

Blakeway, Claire. *Jacques Prévert: Popular French Theatre and Cinema*. Teaneck: Fairleigh Dickinson U.P., 1990. Very solid study of theme, technique and tone, in social context.

Blanchot, Maurice. "L'Honneur des poètes", *L'Arche*, 18-19, août-sept 1946.

Breton, André. Lettre à Jean Duché, *Le Littéraire* (5 oct 1946).

Cinéma 60. Special issue, *Jacques Prévert et Paris,* mai 1960.

Courrière, Yves. *Jacques Prévert,* Paris: Gallimard, 2000. Biography.

Delvaille, Bernard. *"Choses et autres"*, *Combat*, 14 déc 1972.

Europe. Special issue on Prévert, août 1991.

Faure, Michel. *Le Groupe Octobre*. Paris: Bourgois, 1977.

Fiorioli, Elena. "La Poesia di Prévert, simbolo di un'epoca", *Il Cristallo*, XXXIV, 2, Agosto 1994, 95-102.

Gasiglia-Laster, Danièle. *Jacques Prévert*. Biarritz: Séguier, 1986. Compactly biographical, with yet a critical sensitivity that is revealed to the full in her superb coedition of the Pléiade *Oeuvres complètes*.

Gilson, René. *Des mots et merveilles, Jacques Prévert*. Paris: Belfond, 1990. Essentially biographical in treatment.

Greet, Anne Hyde. *Jacques Prévert's Word Games*. Berkeley: U. California P., 1968. A sound analysis of Prévert's language patterns.

Guillot, Gérard. *Les Prévert*. Paris: Seghers, 1966. Biographical.

Heinrich, André. *Album Jacques Prévert*. Paris: Pléiade, 1992. Full of excellent iconography.

Lapprand, Marc. *Trois fous du langage. Vian, Queneau, Prévert*. Presses de l'Université de Nancy, 1993. One or two sound pertinent studies on Prévert.

Laster, Arnaud. *Prévert*. Paris: Hatier, 1972. Compact "profile" of the work by one of the best Prévert critics and coeditor of the superb Pléiade *Oeuvres complètes*.

___. "L'humour complice de l'amour chez Prévert", *Mélusine*, X, 1988, 159-70.

___. "De quoi pourrait se composer une édition critique des textes de Prévert pour le film *Notre Dame de Paris?*, in *Editer des oeuvres médiatiques*. Québec: Université de Laval/CRELIQ, 192, 131-46.

Magazine Littéraire. Dossier Jacques Prévert. Special issue, 155, déc. 1979. Short studies and homage.

Nadeau, Maurice. "Prévert ou l'avènement de la poésie matérialiste", *La Revue Internationale*, 6, 1946, 513-17.

Nau, Peter. "Prévert, Cineast", *Filmkritik*, XXVII, 1983, 347-93.

Parlebas, Pierre. "Le synthème dans les *Paroles* de Prévert", *Poétique*, VII, 1976, 496-510.

Pérez, Michel. *Les Films de Carné*. Paris: Ramsay, 1987. Pertinent discussion of Prévert's long collaboration with Carné.

Picon, Gaëtan. "Une poésie populaire", *Confluences*, 10, mars, 1946, 81-87.

Queneau, Raymond. "Jacques Prévert, le bon génie", *Revue de Paris*, juin 1951, 39-46.

Quéval, Jean. *Jacques Prévert*. Paris: Mercure de France, 1955. Good early study with some emphasis on film work.

Rachline, Michel. *Jacques Prévert: drôle de vie*. Paris: Ramsay, 1981.

Rustenholz, Alain. *Prévert, inventaire*. Paris: Seuil, 1990. A sound descriptive commentary on the full career.

Sadeler, Joël. *À travers Prévert*. Paris: Larousse, 1975.

Sortilèges. Special issue, *Jacques Prévert parmi nous*, 3ᵉ trim., 1953. Full range of early assessments.

Spitzer, Susan. "Prévert's political theatre. Two versions of *La Bataille de Fontenay*", *Theatre Research International*, III, 1, Oct. 1977, 54-65.

Weber, Verena. *Form und Funktion von Sprachspielen. Dargestellt anhand des poetischen Werkes von Prévert*. Fischer, 1980.